With Much Love

Allen

Frances Tenenbaum, Series Editor

HOUGHTON MIFFLIN COMPANY
Boston • New York   1997

Indoor Gardens

Tovah Martin

A complete how-to guide to selecting,
planting, and caring for the best plants for
every indoor landscape

CONTENTS

E veryone should have the pleasure of living with houseplants, coming home in the evening to find a plant waiting, leaning over to smell a fragrant flower first thing in the morning. With houseplants, it is possible to garden no matter where you live, no matter what the season. And the beauty of it is, you don't need outdoor space and you don't need special tools to grow houseplants. All you need is a little expertise. With this book in hand, you will be able to select the right plant for any space in your house. You'll learn all the necessary basics to make your windowsills or artificial light gardens lush with greenery and flowers. You'll learn how to fertilize and repot as well as how to shape standards and handle vines. Furthermore, you'll glean ideas for making plants part of your interior decor, for when they're properly grown and skillfully displayed, plants make wonderful living elements of design.

A grouping of supermarket finds, such as spider plant, asparagus fern, and solanum, can transform a windowsill into an indoor garden.

CHAPTER 1:

LIGHT:
THE DEFINING FACTOR

In a greenhouse or garden center, where all of the houseplants have been growing under ideal conditions, they are the picture of blooming good health. But unless you can duplicate those conditions in your own house, you should resist the urge to pick up the first pretty flower that catches your fancy. If you select a plant on the strength of its deep red leaves, you won't want the foliage to fade to green in your home. If you fall in love with a plant's dark blue blossoms, it will be a great disappointment if the flowers all fall for lack of light.

So before you pick up the pot and put down your money, you need to understand the plant's cultural requirements and think about whether its needs will be met by the living conditions in your home. Before you select a plant, consider where you plan to place it, how warm that location will be, and how often you can take time to visit it with a watering pot. There are thousands of houseplants out there. Some originally grew in tropical forests and will adapt to low-light conditions; others come from the desert and can't live without a lot of sun.

Profiled alone, a Boston fern has an alluring sophistication.
This plant demands high humidity — a bathroom might be the
perfect setting.

THINKING ABOUT EXPOSURE

As you might imagine, the most important factor in a successful indoor garden is light. All plants need light. Some require less sun than others, but none will survive in a dark closet without some sort of artificial light. So it's wise to plan your indoor displays around windows. When you are struck by the urge to garden indoors, before rushing off to the garden center you should assess the available light at each window.

It sounds simple to figure out how much light your windows receive: since the sun rises in the east and sets in the west, you just have to figure out if your window faces north, south, east, or west. As a rule, south-facing windows bask in the most light and can support sun-loving flowering plants such as geraniums, herbs, hibiscus, mandevillas, and many more. Windows that face east or west receive half a day of sun and can nurture plants such as begonias, African violets, and orchids, which require good light but don't demand direct sun. And north-facing windows, which get the least light, can support little besides ferns and other foliage plants.

But other factors also come into play. For example, your south-facing window may be obstructed by the canopy of a shade tree, which will provide an umbrella during summer but allow plenty of light to enter when winter rolls around. Or a neighboring building or a porch or overhang may block the direct sun, making the window the equivalent of an east- or west-facing exposure. Or some foundation plantings may stand between your indoor garden and the essential sunbeams.

If your east or west window looks out on a pond or lake, the incoming light will be intensified, making the sill as bright as one that faces south. Windows facing a cement sidewalk or wall often receive more light than those overlooking a lawn or garden. In short, the direction a window faces — north, south, east, or west — is not the whole answer to the question of how much light it provides. As you monitor your light, notice whether the windows receive direct sun and how long it lasts. And bear in mind that the level and direction of light change with the seasons. At first you'll have to reassess the light situation every few months.

You can do some things to enhance the quality of light coming into a window. First and most obviously, you can wash the panes — a little chore that has

A sunny window in a busy part of the house will benefit from a head-turning flowering plant. Egyptian stars comes in a broad array of blossom colors and blooms throughout the year.

an amazing impact on the intensity of light on the sill. You can wake up early and open the curtains. You can omit curtains entirely or choose sheer fabrics. You can position your plants close to the glass or, if they are getting too much sun, you can move them back. If you are more ambitious, you can trim obstructing foundation plantings or have some lower limbs removed from the trees in your yard. You can summon all your courage and walk next door to ask your neighbor not to park his trailer truck in front of your window garden. When you think about it, it's surprising how much control you can exercise over the light that falls on your houseplants.

SOUTH-FACING WINDOWS

Consider yourself lucky if you have a south-facing window in your home, for by and large, most bloomers will benefit from the direct sun. In fact, many tropical plants, such as pelargoniums (commonly known as geraniums), mandevillas, hibiscus, abutilons, passionflowers, heliotrope, bougainvilleas, brugmansias, and pentas require good light to produce flowers. If a plant refuses to blossom, chances are good that it is not receiving sufficient light; move it to a south-facing window, and it may bud up immediately.

In most parts of the country, plants bask happily in the bright sun of a southern exposure as long as you are careful to furnish water before they wilt. However, in the Southwest and other sunny regions, the light from a south-facing

---

Plants for South-Facing Windows

Abutilon, flowering maple
Acalypha, chenille plant, strawberry firetails
Alstroemeria, Brazilian lily
Bougainvillea, paper flower
Brugmansia, angel's trumpet
Brunfelsia, yesterday-today-and-tomorrow
Cactus, cactus
Cestrum, night-blooming jasmine
Clerodendrum, glory-bower
Crossandra, firecracker flower
Cuphea, Hawaiian heather
Gardenia, gardenia
Heliotropium, heliotrope, cherry pie
Hibiscus, rose of China
Justicia, shrimp plant
Lantana, polecat geranium
Lavandula, lavender

Lobelia, lobelia
Lotus, winged pea
Mandevilla, mandevilla
Manettia, firecracker plant
Ocimum, basil
Passiflora, passionflower
Pentas, Egyptian stars
Pseuderanthemum, amethyst stars
Punica, pomegranate
Rosmarinus, rosemary
Ruellia, trailing velvet plant
Salvia, sage
Stephanotis, Madagascar jasmine
Streptosolen, marmalade plant
Thymus, thyme
Tropaeolum, nasturtium

When light is plentiful, all sorts of sun-worshippers will thrive, including plants normally grown in the garden, such as zonal geraniums and campanula.

window will be too intense during the summer months. It is wise to pull tropical plants back a few feet away before the first signs of scorching occur (the symptoms include white burn markings on the leaves). And south windows in an upper-story city apartment receive an astonishing amount of light. If you have a very bright exposure, move your plants back from the window. Certain plants, such as cacti and succulents, alpines and Mediterranean herbs, are adapted to growing in radiantly bright locations. Even so, any plant will burn if it is suddenly exposed to bright light following a period of darkness. If you've just purchased a succulent from the supermarket, allow it to adapt to the brighter light of your home gradually before exposing it to the full brunt of a bright south-facing window.

During most seasons of the year and in most parts of the country, you should position your plants within two feet of the windowpanes. Not only should the plants be clustered close to the window, but they should be rotated a quarter turn every week so that all sides will benefit equally from the sun. And keep in mind that a hefty plant standing right in front of the window will shade smaller plants placed farther from the light source. If you want to display something bulky directly in front of the panes, cluster plants that prefer lower light in its shadow.

EAST- AND WEST-FACING WINDOWS

Windows that face east or west and receive only about half a day of direct light can still nurture quite an array of houseplants. Actually, in some seasons, east and west windows capture a very generous flow of light. If the window is unobstructed and if you choose plants that will perform without intense sun, you can enjoy just as many blossoms as you'd have on a southern sill. And plants grown with half a day of light require a fraction of the effort as far as upkeep is concerned. When the sun isn't streaming in, you don't have to make such frequent visits with the watering can and you don't have to fertilize as often. And your plants will not outgrow their pots so quickly.

Some plants prefer lower light levels. Episcias, begonias, African violets, gloxinias, columneas, plectranthus, coleus, hoyas, citrus, orchids, jasmines, and camellias will grow lushly, blossom, and be fruitful in an east or west window. In fact, all of these plants may scorch under more intense light. In winter you might place them in a south-facing window without problems. But when summer comes, with its longer days and more intense light, plants that prefer partial sun will begin to show signs of stress. Leaves may curl, fade, or become dwarfed, and growth may halt or become lethargic. When a plant just doesn't seem to be performing as it should, incorrect light intensity is often the culprit. And summertime isn't the only season to be on your guard against sunburn. Often, plants that like partial sun will do fine in an east or west window until autumn, when shade trees suddenly shed their foliage, exposing your windows to harsher rays. Then the plants inside may begin to protest — scorching, shriveling, curling their leaves, and complaining in other discreet ways.

Plants for East- and West-Facing Windows

Alocasia, elephant's ear plant
Anthurium, flamingo flower
Begonia (rex, angel-wing,
    rhizomatous, tuberous,
    wax)
Caladium
Calathea, peacock plant
Camellia
Canna, Indian-shot

Citrus, orange, lemon, lime,
    grapefruit
Clivia, clivia
Coffea, coffee
Columnea, dragon flower
Costus, spiral ginger
Episcia, flame violet
Fuchsia, lady's eardrops
Hoya, Indian rope plant

Jasminum, jasmine
Mentha, mint
Mitriostigma, African gardenia
Murraya, orange jasmine
Orchids
Saintpaulia, African violet
Sinningia, gloxinia
Solenostemon, coleus
Viola, pansy, violet

Orchids, begonias, amaryllis, and gesneriads all prefer the partial sun of an east- or west-facing window. Clustering the plants increases the humidity in the immediate area, another requirement of these plants.

Although the indoor garden may seem unconnected to the outdoors, in reality your home environment is closely linked with and affected by nature's rhythms. Become attuned to the ways that seasonal changes alter the habitat of your windowsill. Watch your plants' body language. Those that are hungering for more light will lean toward the window in search of sun. Plants that are receiving too much sun turn away from the light source and blanch. It is important to react to such signs of distress immediately; nevertheless, when you're moving plants to a new location, do it gradually. You shouldn't suddenly take a plant from a half-shady east or west window and place it beneath a skylight on a sun-drenched day.

Certain plants will not do well in less than full sun, but others are more flexible. With a little careful planning, you can often persuade sun-worshipers to thrive and blossom on an east- or west-facing windowsill. Maximize the available light by strategically placing the plants close to the window. Rather than siting them on a low plant stand, set the pots level with the sill so that the bottom leaves can bask in the sun. Make certain that none of the plants is hiding in another's shadows. And be sure to rotate each pot a quarter turn once a week to expose all sides to the sun.

Although you can often convince sun-lovers to blossom even without direct sun, the plants will be a little lankier and will probably need pruning more often than their counterparts grown on a southern sill, especially in winter or during extended periods of cloudy weather. Pruning will maintain the plant's stature so that the flowers stand at eye level rather than scraping the ceiling. All upright plants should be pruned; we will explore pruning techniques more fully in the next chapter.

Although plants in south-facing windows often need daily watering, especially in summer, those grown in an east or west window don't demand as much attention with the watering can. Stubbornly following a strict watering schedule will doom any indoor garden to failure, especially one in an east or west window. It's disastrous to water every morning — wait until the soil is dry. If the soil is still damp when you're checking your plants before you leave for the day, let them wait until the next morning. Keep in mind that in an east- or west-facing window, the plant is not likely to wilt. And if the foliage does flag slightly, it will recover the moment it's moistened.

During the summer, when the fireplace isn't in use, a bird's nest fern fills this low-light space with majestic fronds.

NORTH-FACING WINDOWS

Even if you have only north-facing windows, you can still grow houseplants. Granted, you won't be able to entertain the bounty of blossoms that someone blessed with a southern exposure can cultivate. The best method of dealing with a north window is to select plants that prefer low light rather than trying and failing to grow flowers. Design a windowsill arrangement that hinges on foliar patterns and balances different shades of green. Work with textures. Go for the forest look.

As we know from dentists' offices and banks, plants in low-light locations can be very blah. You are undoubtedly weary of bumping into philodendrons, draceanas, dieffenbachias, and their ilk in shopping malls and other windowless spaces. Even if you don't want to venture beyond the foliage plants that can be found in the supermarket, you can display your plants creatively and thus improve their image. You'll be surprised what a fancy pot can do to create drama. Even the old Victorian standbys, famed for staying alive in shadowed corners where nothing else will thrive, can be featured with a novel slant. A sansevieria or aspidistra can be strikingly architectural when potted in a majestic urn and silhouetted against a window. It's all in the packaging, the presentation. Foliage plants may not grow exuberantly or offer the drama of flowers, but if thoughtfully presented, they can be stunning.

Beyond the choices found in the average office or mall, there are plenty of plants that are willing to grow in a north-facing window. Ferns are available in such a wide variety of leaf shapes, textures, and sizes that you could easily base a display solely on them. Clustered together, they give each other humidity, which is a crucial factor for ferns. And because they love dampness, ferns are happy in the tropical atmosphere of a bathroom. In the living room you might grow ferns under a glass cloche, in a terrarium, or in a waterless aquarium to raise the humidity. Tropical ferns such as *Nephrolepis* (sword and Boston ferns), *Davallia* (footed ferns), *Cyrtomium* (holly ferns), *Doodia,* and *Blechnum* are all easy to cultivate, growing luxuriantly and sending their fiddleheads stretching upward in normal household climates. *Adiantum* (maidenhair fern) is slightly more challenging, but a bathroom with evenly toasty temperatures and a frequently used shower will keep the humidity sufficiently high that even maidenhairs remain lush. Similarly, mosses such as *Selaginella* look truly lavish in a windowsill, espe-

Sansevieria certainly won't bloom in a north-facing window, but even without the flowers, its stately leaves have a certain architectural grandeur. And it grows in low light where nothing else will thrive.

Although a north-facing window can't support flowers, an array of ferns, philodendrons, and marantas provides plenty of interest with their combined foliage.

cially if their fronds are encouraged to climb up a topiary frame or drape over the sides of a container to resemble a woodland rockery. Both ferns and mosses require frequent watering as well as humid air. When those requisites are met, they create a unique alternative to the foliage plants that are usually seen in north-facing windows.

Peperomias and pileas of all descriptions would be glad to brighten up your north-facing sill, and they require little care and pruning. Ivies are happy in low light, and they need not be boring. Not only are they available in all sorts of leaf shapes, ranging from heart-shaped to lacy, and varying in size from large to less than an inch in diameter, but they feature colors and patterns far beyond plain green. Leaves may be marbled, mottled, streaked, or edged and bicolored with silver, cream, or gold. Some have a hint of rose toward the leaf's heart. There is no plant more affable, more willing to perform under trying conditions. Use ivies to edge indoor window boxes or cascade from shelves, or train them to climb any frame you can find. Hearts, wreaths, and globes are always popular, but be cre-

Plants for North-Facing Windows

Aspidistra, barbershop plant

Blechnum, tree fern

Cyrtomium, holly fern

Davallia, footed fern

Dieffenbachia, dumbcane

Doodia, hacksaw fern

Dracaena, dracaena

Hedera helix, ivy

Monstera, swiss cheese plant

Nephrolepis, sword fern, Boston fern

Philodendron

Sansevieria, rattlesnake plant

ative — anything from a stick trellis to a tennis racket can be employed for the purpose. With a little encouragement, your ivy will quickly camouflage whatever frame you provide for it.

If your north-facing window suggests the feeling of a forest, work with that mood and hide your pots in wooden baskets or rustic cachepots. Any container can be made into a cachepot by adding a plastic lining. I've seen containers woven of grapevines or covered with pine cones or studded with seashells, made to resemble birds' nests, hollowed tree trunks, or squirrels' holes.

For a different feeling entirely, you might jazz up the greenery in your north-facing window with colorfully glazed terra cotta pots, which are most effective when they're not competing with flowers. Or, if your parlor is formal and accented by antiques, select a pot with a crackle or faux-marble finish. Look for containers with intriguing contours and combine them artistically to complement one another.

Any room with a window can and should entertain plants. Don't leave your sun porch empty just because it has no heat. Let the space be filled by hardy evergreen ferns such as the Christmas fern. In a chilly alcove you can grow deciduous bonsai, dwarf conifers, alpines, and heathers. Bring the beauty of nature into your home. French doors, bay windows, bathrooms, pantry sills — any place where light is available can harbor houseplants.

CHAPTER 2:

ARTIFICIAL LIGHT

Even if your home has only north-facing windows and receives insufficient natural light, even if you live in a dense forest or on the bottom floor of a skyscraper in the city, you can still enjoy houseplants. By using an artificial light source, you can produce blossoms in even the darkest room.

USES FOR ARTIFICIAL LIGHTS

How can you tell when artificial lights are necessary? If your houseplants flag and grow spindly, the problem is probably insufficient natural light. One solution is to select plants that are happiest in low light — but not everyone wants to be limited to aspidistras and sansevierias. Artificial lights allow anyone, no matter where they live, to enjoy the beauty and satisfaction of a wide variety of house-plants.

Even in the brightest home, the light available indoors is only a fraction of the wattage that plants receive in a sunny garden outside. With fluorescent tubes,

Miniature plants that grow happily in a terrarium, such as polka dot plants, selaginella mosses, and nerve plant, will thrive under artificial lights.

you can supplement your supply of natural light. If you have been unable to coax a Martha Washington geranium into blossom in your west-facing window, you can prep the plant under artificial lights until buds begin to swell, then bring it proudly into the public arena. Along with inducing unwilling plants to flower, you can cajole many sun-loving plants into blooming more vigorously by augmenting the natural sunbeams, especially during the winter.

Artificial lights can also be employed to alter a plant's natural rhythm. Increased light will keep some plants growing and alter their blooming schedule. You can trick spring bulbs into blooming when they wouldn't normally flower and convince summer bloomers to perform when the days outdoors are still short. Plants that go soundly asleep at a certain time of year, such as tuberous begonias and oxalis, cannot be persuaded to vary their slumber routine. But you can tease some perennials and herbs not to slip into dormancy and even grow basil at the time of year when it normally slumps.

However, in the case of many winter bloomers, twelve hours of light may prevent bud development. Poinsettias, kalanchoes, winter-blooming jasmine, Christmas cacti, and Thanksgiving cacti may fail to flower if they receive too much light. Interestingly, night-blooming plants such as the night-blooming jasmine, *Cestrum nocturnum,* will not alter their cycle when they're grown under lights. Oblivious to the fact that lights are shining, they continue to open after dusk.

You can also raise seedlings or propagate cuttings under the gentle light of fluorescent tubes. Most artificial lights supply additional heat, which seedlings and cuttings appreciate. And fledgling plants prefer the low-stress environment provided by controlled light.

TYPES OF LIGHTS

Until recently, the most commonly employed artificial lights were long fluorescent tubes plugged into ballasts. Because the tubes had to be within 2 feet of the plants, they were generally built into carts designed especially for the purpose. "Grow carts" are convenient, there's no doubt about it. Sophisticated models feature large plastic trays to catch watering spills. And if you cannot regularly attend to your plants' needs for water, you can fit the trays of the cart with mats that

A floral cart is the most common means of providing plants with artificial light. It's a convenient way to accommodate and care for a carpet of small plants.

wick up the water and keep the roots evenly moist. The more sophisticated models feature adjustable light fixtures that can be raised and lowered to accommodate the height of your plants. If you are starting seedlings indoors, this is a crucial element.

However, grow carts aren't the only possibility. You can easily create your own artificial light setup by installing a fluorescent tube ballast on the underside of a shelf. Some gardeners install fluorescent lights for plants in sections of their bookshelves. If you shield the light from view with a valance, the scene doesn't seem artificial at all. Or you can invest in a flood lamp made specifically for plants.

The field of artificial-light gardening has come a long way from those purple tubes that shed an eerie light throughout the room. And there's no need to resort to high-powered high-intensity-discharge (HID) sodium lamps, which cast an orange-red glow reminiscent of street lamps, accompanied by a loud hum. Newer light sources can be blissfully unobtrusive.

When you're using artificial lights, whether on a cart or in a free-standing fixture, you should select fluorescent tubes manufactured specifically for plants. Leaves require red and blue light to thrive, while orange-red light boosts bud development. Most indoor gardeners opt for two different types of tubes hung in tandem on a ballast. The tubes come in standard sizes — 24 inches long, offering 20 watts of light, or 48 inches long, furnishing 40 watts. Virginie Elbert, a New York City apartment gardener who is an expert in the field of light gardening, recommends the common and relatively inexpensive combination of a Warm-White fluorescent hung beside a Cool-White one. "Warm" and "cool" refer to the color of the light, not the temperature of the fluorescent tube. Originally developed for office buildings, these tubes are readily available from several different manufacturers. Other recommended fluorescent lights include Gro-Lux, Vitalite, and PowerTwist. Sometimes inexpensive flood lamps (which are often merely incandescent bulbs buffered with a coat of blue paint) are marketed for use with houseplants, but they are not effective.

No matter which brand of fluorescent tube you choose, you'll need to plug into a ballast, which should conform to Underwriters Laboratory (UL) standards and be approved for use near water. To best distribute the light, ballasts should be hung horizontally over a cluster of plants. They are most effective when fitted with a reflector painted white or cream.

The newest innovation is the Wonderlite®, which is a 160-watt, self-ballasted flood lamp that provides the wide spectrum of light that houseplants require. This oversized 5-inch bulb, consisting of a mercury-arc tube, phosphor-coated glass, and an incandescent filament, can be inserted into any household socket rated for 150 to 160 watts. Many people plug them into overhead track lighting sockets. And they can successfully nurture plants 8 feet away.

Plants must be much closer to fluorescent tubes to gain the benefit of their light. You'll probably have to experiment to find out how far each plant should sit from the tubes. As a rule, the lights should be no more than 6 to 8 inches above most plants. However, plants such as succulents that demand a lot of light

Although they become tall, cattleya orchids are often grown under artificial lights until the buds begin to swell. Then they are brought out onto center stage.

Plants Easily Grown under Fluorescent Lights

Begonias (rex, rhizomatous, wax)
Biophytum, sensitive plant
Columnea, dragon flower
Mikania
Miniature roses
Orchids
Peperomia
Pilea, cat's tongue plant
Rondeletia, Panama rose

Saintpaulia, African violet
Saxifraga sarmentosa, strawberry begonia
Scaevola, fan flower
Serissa, snow rose
Streptocarpus, Cape primrose
Tetranema, Mexican foxglove
Tropaeolum, nasturtium
Viola, violet, pansy

should be grown within 3 inches of the tubes. And plants that prefer lower light, such as begonias, can be placed as far as 12 inches from the light source.

No matter which brand you select, you should not keep your artificial lights glowing 24 hours a day; most plants cannot utilize more than 12 to 14 hours of light daily. Plants with extremely high light demands, such as succulents and certain orchids, should be illuminated for 16 hours. The easiest method of control is to run your lights on a timer that automatically switches the lights on and off.

GROWING PLANTS UNDER ARTIFICIAL LIGHT

If you're new to houseplants, artificial-light gardening is a good way to begin your foray into the field. You can count on 12 hours of light daily whether it's cloudy or sunny outside, so it's easier to follow a fixed watering schedule. However, you should still monitor your plants for dryness. Variations in the indoor temperature and humidity will affect how often they need water. When your central heating system goes on, plants under lights are bound to dry out more frequently. In winter you may have to water plants under artificial light more often than their counterparts in natural light. In summer artifically lighted plants may dry out less frequently than those on a windowsill. Overwatering can be disastrous under lights, because if one plant falls prey to a fungal disease brought on by overwatering, the problem will spread like wildfire to its neighbors clustered nearby.

Although you may have initially placed your plants at the proper distance from the fluorescent tubes, they will expand upward. Monitor the plants to make certain that they haven't gotten too close to the lights, which can cause leaves to become burned or distorted. The heat from the light may also adversely affect the plant's growth. As plants gain height, you can adjust the fluorescent tube if it's on a movable ballast, or you can prune back the plant.

When you cluster plants closely together under fluorescent lights, the humidity in the area increases, which can be a definite bonus for indoor gardeners. However, pests such as fungus gnats and slugs, which are fond of damp growing conditions, may proliferate. Preventive measures are particularly imperative in a close-knit community. When you spray for insect control, be certain to penetrate all the nooks and crannies of compact plants. Check the leaves and soil in your light garden often, and keep plants groomed, removing any rotting matter in the vicinity. Remove spent flowers and dead leaves immediately. If you are growing plants in a basement, mildew can be a problem. Fans are particularly helpful under artificial lights.

Aside from these cautionary notes, growing plants under artificial light is basically similar to growing them on a windowsill, except that you needn't worry when the weather turns cloudy for a week. You're likely to see flowers when natural light gardeners are still praying for buds. At greater expense, perhaps, but with a fraction of the work.

CHAPTER 3:

SELECTING THE PLANTS

F ew activities are more pleasant on a dreary winter day than spending time (and money) in a greenhouse buying plants for your indoor garden. This chapter gives some guidelines to help you make the right decisions. The first requirement, as you've already learned, is to match the plant to the light conditions in your home. Beyond that, here are some other considerations: Is a small cutting best, or is it wiser to choose a full-grown specimen? How can you tell if the plant that catches your eye is healthy? Should you buy a plant with blossoms? Or is it best to select one that is growing robustly but has no buds?

DECIDING ON SIZE

When you mentally designed your indoor garden, you probably had plants of a certain size in mind. Now is the time to decide whether you want to nurture your plants to that size yourself or buy them fully grown. The most obvious factor in your decision is money. A large plant will be more expensive than the same variety in a smaller size; after all, several years probably elapsed while the nurs-

Look for plants that have been pinched to encourage branching. This white tiddly-winks will continue in prime condition for several months.

Some plants, such as palms, bird of paradise, euphorbias, and bromeliads, reach their stride and look stunning only at maturity. Rather than buying them small and waiting for years, you might as well invest in sizable plants.

ery grew those plants to maturity, during which time they had to be fed, watered, repotted, pruned, and kept warm. Do you want to repot your young plants several times as they grow? And do you have the patience to wait while the plant reaches its mature size? Before you decide to be a do-it-yourselfer and save money, consider the work entailed.

Some plants, such as ferns, take a long time to reach maturity, so it is a good idea to purchase them full grown if you want your windowsill to look its best in the near future. Likewise, orchids should be purchased as blooming-sized plants. While you may not want to spend the money for a phalaenopsis with a 5-foot-long flower spike, you won't want to fuss with an orchid straight from the seedling flask either. And speaking of seedlings, exotic houseplants are occasionally featured in seed catalogs. It seems like such a good deal — twenty-five seeds for $6.95. But keep in mind that tropical plants take several years to bloom from seed, and there's a lot of attrition along the way. Bougainvilleas, camellias, citrus, and many other hardwood plants take their jolly good time before reaching blooming size. For your own satisfaction, start with a plant large enough to look attractive and blossom within a reasonable amount of time.

But bigger is not always better. Many plants, such as begonias, geraniums, abutilons, plectranthus, and dwarf fuchsias, look great when they're small. You can purchase a 4-inch pot and feel confident that your plant will look splendid and bloom even before you repot it. In fact, peperomias and other dwarf plants look best when they're still in their cute youthful stage.

There are other reasons to buy small plants. If you're buying one to shape into a standard or some other form of topiary, it's advisable to start training the plant early in its career. After all, it's not easy to teach an old plant new tricks. Once a sprawling plant has started to cascade, it becomes difficult or impossible to coax its main stem up to form a weeping standard. When you plan to train plants, it's best to purchase fledglings in $2\frac{1}{2}$-inch pots (sometimes called liners).

Compact plants will travel more comfortably than larger specimens. If you find a rarity at a specialist nursery in Idaho and want to carry it on the plane back to New Jersey, choose the smallest plant you can find. Many specialist mail-order nurseries ship only in small containers to minimize damage in transport. And after they arrive, young plants often adjust to change more readily than older ones that have lots of foliage to support.

Even as small cuttings, New Guinea hybrid impatiens are dappled with blossoms.

FINDING HEALTHY PLANTS

When you go on a plant-buying spree, always survey the greenhouse or garden center for the general overall health of the plants in residence. Do you see bugs flitting around? Are the plants wilted, sunburned, or otherwise stressed? If the place doesn't have a healthy appearance, go no further. Leave empty-handed.

Even if the greenhouse has a healthy appearance, look at a plant closely before you buy it. First of all, look for insects. Examine the soft tips of new growth and the leaf petioles for aphids — that's where they love to wedge. Turn the leaves upside down and examine the undersides for aphids as well. It isn't difficult to get rid of these pests, but why introduce the risk of infesting your other plants? Other pests to check for are mealybugs, which look like wads of cotton; red spider mites, which are barely visible — look for tiny red specks and telltale webs on the undersides of the leaves; whiteflies, little white bugs that take wing when you jostle the foliage; and scale — check for brown bumps on the stems and leaves. If you're in doubt about the plant's condition, ask a nursery person to examine it. Not all extraneous bumps and blobs on leaves and stems are bug-related. Certain plants, such as passifloras and ipomoeas, secrete a substance onto their leaf surfaces that looks similar to an insect egg mass. And not all insects are detrimental. Nowadays, many nurseries are turning to beneficial insects as a means of pest control.

Just to be on the safe side, many gardeners quarantine their new plants for a few weeks before adding them to a thriving indoor garden. If no problems show up in that time, you can then put your new purchases with your other plants without fear of infestation.

When you buy plants, check them for disease problems. Rotting stems and mottled foliage are never good signs. If you find any sort of ringlike markings, either concentric rings or round discolored spots, avoid that plant as well as its neighbors in the nursery. Such problems can spread like a plague. Not quite so serious, but also reason for concern, are yellowed leaves, which generally indicate stress (unless, of course, you're purchasing the golden form of winter-blooming jasmine or some other yellow-variegated plant). In short, avoid plants that don't seem to be thriving. Trust your instincts.

By the same token, when your Aunt Matilda offers to send you home after Thanksgiving with a piece of her favorite night-blooming cereus, politely demur if the plant is covered with mealybugs. Or, if refusing might hurt her feelings, quietly discard the cuttings after you've pulled out of her driveway.

Even when you make every effort to choose a healthy plant, problems sometimes begin after a plant arrives in your care. If a pest infestation erupts within a few days of purchase, seek redress from the place you bought it. And make sure the insects haven't spread to the neighboring plants. If a plant simply looks mopey, the problem is not likely to be disease but merely homesickness: its new environment is unfamiliar. Give it time. After a few days, it may perk up with no intervention on your part. However, if the plant continues to suffer, you should first check climatic factors; the humidity level may be too low or a hot-air vent may be blowing on the foliage.

You can grow palms from seed, but many years will elapse before the plant is worthy of display.

WHAT TO LOOK FOR IN A HOUSEPLANT

Beyond the obvious concerns about size and health, there are other factors to consider when selecting a plant. First, look for one with good branching. Although the abutilon with one slender stalk and a blossom at the top may be tempting because it's already in flower, you would be wiser to choose a specimen that has been pinched to encourage many stems and, ultimately, more flowers. Pinched plants may look squat right now, but they promise a bounty of growth. Buy for long-lasting future beauty rather than immediate pleasure.

Another reason not to fall for a plant in flower, even one that is branching prolifically, is that it may not adjust to a new environment as readily. Buds tend to drop when you move a plant from place to place. Hibiscus, serissas, and malpighias are particularly sensitive to being shuffled. A newly developed orchid spire may arrive at your house safely, but a long spire carrying buds that are swollen and ready to pop will be very fragile indeed. By the same token, citrus plants often drop their fruit when you put them in a new home. If possible, let the plant complete the gestation period from bud set to ripened fruit all in one place.

Hanging-basket plants sold at the supermarket often look to be in prime condition. You might find an 8- or 10-inch pot of tradescantia, bridal veil, or fuchsia that looks irresistible — in full flower, dense and leafy. However, after a week or so, it begins to look pale and straggly, for you bought it at its peak of splendor. In the long run, it's better to select a plant that's just on the verge of full bloom. Bring it home and keep it well nourished and watered. And when its moment of glory begins to pass, shear it back to encourage another flush of growth. Hanging-basket plants have a tendency to decline after a while if you don't give their stems a stern pruning.

CARING FOR YOUR NEW HOUSEPLANT

You can help ensure the success of a newly purchased plant by giving it a little special care when it first arrives in your home. As I mentioned earlier, the transition period can be traumatic. But you can lessen the shock. If the plant was sitting in a dark corner of the supermarket when it caught your fancy, don't put it in a sunny window on a bright day. Eventually, it can go there, but give it an east- or west-facing sill while it becomes accustomed to the brighter light.

Generally, the rule when you first adopt a plant is to do everything in moderation. If it is wilted when it comes home, give it a drink but don't drench it. Wait a few weeks while it becomes acclimatized before fertilizing. And when you do fertilize, you should start by diluting the plant food, then gradually work up to a full-course meal. Even if a new plant is bursting out of its container, don't repot it for a couple of weeks. Then put it in a pot only one size larger, no matter how tightly cramped the roots were before.

Always check a plant's roots shortly after adopting it to make certain that they are healthy and that the soil is appropriate. Unfortunately, plants are often sold in soils that will not sustain them for long. The soil may be close to cement in consistency, or it may have too much sand or peat or none whatsoever. If your new purchase is only a temporary adornment, such as a pot of tulips or daffodils whose bulbs you will discard later, there's no need to correct the soil. But if you expect a long-term healthy relationship with your houseplant, change the soil. Take it out of its pot, remove any soil that will come free without traumatizing the roots, and replace the soil with a houseplant potting soil. Most soils sold for the purpose at garden centers will do a fine job. In most cases the plant can be returned to the same size pot that it came in.

While the plant is out of its pot, check to make sure the roots are healthy. Are they white and firm or brown and shriveled? Remove any damaged or dead roots, and look for root mealybugs — cottony masses around the edges of the soil. Root mealybug is difficult to combat and can spread easily to neighboring plants, so you should discard any plant that is infested.

Now is the time to think about how you will grow your new plant. If you want a fancier container, toss the plastic pot and find a good terra cotta one instead. If it's a climber, look for a trellis that might be appropriate. Start thinking creatively. And make your new plant part of the family.

CHAPTER 4:

ESSENTIAL INDOOR GARDENING SKILLS

I f you want your indoor garden to be a flower-filled, lush, green botanical paradise, you will need to master a few simple skills. All plants have certain basic needs that must be met if they are to survive. Light and water are the most important requirements, of course, but plants also need food, a certain level of humidity, occasional repotting, pruning, and protection from insects and disease. Unlike the plants in your outdoor garden, your houseplants have to depend on you for everything.

The key to the success of most houseplants is that they've been selected for their ability to do well in typical home conditions. Over the years, people have learned how to grow these particular plants indoors. If you choose a suitable location for your plants and give them the care they require, it's very likely they will thrive.

Straggly stems, extraneous branches, and yellowed leaves should all be clipped off regularly to maintain discipline in your indoor garden.

WATERING

Many indoor gardeners tend to water their houseplants too heavily, especially in midwinter when there's nothing else to occupy a gardener's attention. Instead of watering on a fixed schedule, monitor your plants for signs of thirst. Most plants prefer to dry out before drinks are furnished again. When the soil is continually soggy, the roots suffocate and go stagnant. You can avoid this problem easily by watering only when the soil is fairly dry to the touch.

Rather than watering by the calendar, respond to the weather conditions. During hot, sunny weather in summer, plants sitting in a south-facing window may dry out every day. Check them often. During a spell of wet winter weather, a week may slip by before your houseplants become thirsty. But sun isn't the only factor. When you turn up your thermostat and the furnace comes on at regular intervals, the soil dries out more often. When conditions are cooler you'll need to make less frequent visits with the watering can.

Learning to tell when to water is a skill that may take a little practice. Experts can tell at a glance when a plant needs a drink. But beginners should test their plants to decide when to water. The weight method works for many people: pick up the plant first when the soil is dry and then when it has just been watered. You'll soon be able to discern the difference in weight between saturated soil and soil in need of water. Or you can poke your finger about a half inch into the soil to find out if it is moist below the surface. If it is not, the plant is ready to be watered. Some folks prefer to poke a pencil into the soil. If it comes up with soil clinging to the sharpened point, the plant isn't ready for a drink. You may notice that the soil on top turns a lighter color when it is dry, but surface dryness is not always a reliable indicator of the soil condition down where the roots are. It's safer to judge by sampling the soil below the surface.

Plants in serious need of repotting may require frequent watering. When a plant has outgrown its container, there is scant soil to soak up moisture and many thirsty roots competing for a drink. If you repot the plant, you won't have to make so many visits with the watering can. On the other hand, if a plant is in a pot that is too generous, the soil stays soggy because the roots cannot possibly lap up all the moisture that surrounds them.

The type of soil and the plant's original habitat also govern how often water-ing is required. Soils with a lot of sand dry out more frequently than those composed primarily of peat or sphagnum moss. Plants that originally came from desert, alpine, and Mediterranean regions prefer less water than those adapted to jungles or the tropics. As a rule, broad-leaved plants dry out faster than their smaller-leaved counterparts.

Some gardeners assume that a plant is ready to be watered when it wilts. Granted, wilting is often an indication that the soil is dry. But when the sun shines intensely after a period of cloudy weather, plants sometimes wilt whether or not they are ready to be watered. Wilting may also be a sign of soggy soil, root disease, or a root insect infestation. In these cases applying more water simply worsens the situation. If a plant wilts, check the level of moisture in the soil before deciding to water.

When you've decided that a plant is definitely thirsty, the best method of furnishing a drink is to slowly fill the pot to its rim and let the moisture soak down. Of course, this method is practicable only if your plant has been properly potted so that there's at least a half inch of space between the top of the soil and the rim. When a pot is totally filled with soil, there's no space to hold water.

A watering can for indoors should be small enough and have a spout sufficiently slender so anyone can easily aim and pour.

Although overwatering is more common, underwatering can also wreak havoc. Parched soil will not absorb moisture properly unless the root ball is soaked in a bucket of water or in the sink for a few minutes. Soil is like a sponge; when it becomes too dry, water flows down the edges of the pot and straight out the drainage hole without actually moistening the soil. If you have been watering properly, the moisture will seep slowly down to the bottom, thoroughly wetting the roots.

Drainage holes are essential in any pot. And the saucer should be emptied of excess water a few minutes after you've quenched the plant's thirst. Some plants, such as African violets, must be watered carefully so droplets don't linger on the sensitive leaves. Aim your water spout at the soil rather than the foliage, or water the plant from below, filling the saucer, letting the water soak up into the root ball, then emptying any remaining moisture after an hour or so.

Think twice before adding decorative top dressings to a pot, for they can confuse the issue of when to water. When moss or pebbles hide the soil from view, it can be confounding even for an expert to ascertain whether the soil is dry. And living moss on top of the soil may lap up water and hold it around the base of the plant, causing stem rot.

TEMPERATURE

Some like it hot, some like it cold, but most houseplants thrive in the same sort of living conditions that you prefer. Even tropicals, which in their native habitats enjoy quite warm daytime temperatures, are happiest with a slightly cool resting period at night; 55 or 60 degrees Fahrenheit is ideal for most plants. During

---

Plants That Prefer Temperatures above 65 Degrees

Alocasia, elephant's ear plant
Begonias
Bougainvillea
Brunfelsia, yesterday-today-and-
  tomorrow
Clerodendrum, glory-bower
Columnea, dragon flower
Episcia, flame violet
Gardenia

Jasminum sambac 'Maid of Orleans',
  jasmine
Justicia, Brazilian plume flower
Mandevilla
Nematanthus, goldfish plant
Sinningia, gloxinia
Saintpaulia, African violet
Streptocarpella
Streptocarpus, Cape primrose

> ## Plants That Need Cool Temperatures (below 55 degrees at night) to Form Buds
>
> *Acacia,* acacia
> Camellia
> *Cestrum,* night-blooming jasmine
> *Genista,* Canary Island broom
> *Hebe,* hebe
> *Hermannia,* honeybells
>
> *Jasminum polyanthum,*
>   winter-blooming jasmine
> *Lotus,* winged pea
> *Osteospermum,* osteospermum
> *Viola,* violet, pansy

the day, a rise in temperature of 10 to 20 degrees, as the sun or the furnace warms the atmosphere, is fine. If the temperature rises more than that, most houseplants will remain content as long as they are afforded a resting period at night.

Of course, there are exceptions. Begonias, bougainvilleas, and members of the African violet family prefer temperatures that never fall below 65 degrees Fahrenheit. If it gets colder they express their displeasure by dropping leaves and slipping into dormancy just when you want them to perform. And at the other extreme, acacias, Carolina jasmine, cytisus, and winter-blooming jasmine will not form buds unless they are given a period of 50-degree or cooler temperatures. If a winter-blooming plant fails to set buds during its appointed season, it may be because the temperature is too warm. Turn the thermostat down at night or move the plants to a cool room.

HUMIDITY

During the winter, when heating systems are running full blast, the atmospheric humidity in many homes drops to very low levels. If the cat's fur stands on end when you run your hand down its back and the piano continually goes out of tune, you can safely assume that the air is too dry for your houseplants. Wood-burning stoves are the worst culprits for depleting atmospheric humidity, followed by forced-hot-air systems. The least detrimental type of heating for your houseplants is a hot-water system.

The simplest way to increase the atmospheric humidity immediately around your plants is to cluster them together on a pebble tray.

It's amazing how rapidly plants react to low atmospheric humidity. The first symptom is yellowing leaves or browning leaf edges. This is eventually followed by a dramatic amount of leaf drop, which will lead sooner or later to total collapse. Even if the general humidity level is reasonably good, your plants will suffer if a hot-air vent or radiator shaft blows directly on their foliage.

Of course, there are ways to correct the situation. In the case of the offending heat vent, you'd be wise to relocate your plants. Overall low humidity is somewhat more complicated to remedy. Humidity rises when the furnace is not continually pouring heat, so some houseplant aficionados lower the thermostat a little during the winter and wear sweaters around the house. However, if you're not prepared to rough it for your plants, try adding moisture to the air.

The best way to add humidity around your houseplants is to install a good humidifier; inexpensive versions often merely spray water droplets in the imme-

The Victorians invented the Wardian case, a glorified terrarium, to give plants needed humidity. A propagator can be enlisted for the same purpose.

diate area, wetting the floor but failing to put moisture into the air. More effective models raise the humidity over a broader area. Placing a tray of water to evaporate on top of a radiator or on the wood stove can also help. Or you can set your plants on a moisture tray. Spread pebbles to the depth of one inch on the bottom of a shallow tray, add a half inch of water, and set your plants on the pebbles. Be sure to keep the water level below the pebbles (never allow your plant pots to wallow in water) and refill the tray as the water evaporates. Of course, any old cookie pan will do for a moisture tray, but you can find some rather fancy units that perform this function. Copper trays equipped with waffle-shaped plastic inserts as a substitute for pebbles are the state of the art when it comes to increasing humidity.

Clustering plants together is another way to raise the humidity in the immediate vicinity. An extreme but highly successful tactic is to place all your plants

If your air is very dry, a terrarium can provide the humidity your plants need.
However, the plants confined to such tight quarters must remain extremely compact.

in an aquarium or terrarium. More elaborate still, you could purchase a Wardian case, which is a piece of Victorian furniture with a giant terrarium on top. Within your glass-encased area, you can set up all sorts of scenes. Some people lay pebble pathways around miniature ferns, begonias, orchids, or gesneriads, composing a Lilliputian world surrounded by crystal. An equally dramatic and effective means of increasing humidity is to install an indoor fountain or other water feature. At one time fountains were used solely in outdoor gardens, but recently they have become more common indoors as people approach their interior garden spaces from a design-oriented stance.

Not all methods of increasing the humidity work. One common practice that is not particularly effective is to fill a spray bottle with water and spritz your plants once or twice daily. Misting is a very temporary fix, for it raises the moisture in the air for a only a matter of seconds; then the droplets linger on the foliage, inviting bacterial infections. You would have to spritz your plants every fifteen minutes, night and day, to effectively raise the humidity level in their surroundings. Choose one of the less labor-intensive approaches.

REPOTTING

When a plant outgrows its pot you should feel proud, for nature is patting you on the back, demonstrating that your efforts have been well received. Although plants should never be repotted until the roots fill the current container, there are some clues that will tell you a plant is ready to graduate. First, the foliage will probably wilt more rapidly than usual because so many roots are jammed into a small area. Furthermore, the foliage is likely to have paled to a lighter shade of green. When you notice these subtle hints, turn the pot over to see if roots are protruding from the drainage hole. However, even if you have a strong hunch that your plant is ready to be repotted, you should not perform the deed until you've removed it and examined the root system. If the container is crowded with roots, the plant is ready to be moved into a larger container. This need not be done just before a season of slow growth, for in dormancy, the roots don't need more room. For example, if you notice in the autumn that your rosemary is craving a larger container, wait and repot it in spring when the herb is on the verge of an active growth cycle.

It doesn't harm a plant in the least to expose and examine its roots for a few minutes to see what is going on underground. Before removing the pot, water the plant and let the moisture sink down. Then turn the pot upside down, tap the rim on the edge of your work table, and let the root ball fall into your waiting palm. Removing the pot from a larger plant is often a two-person job. If a container is too large and heavy to be turned upside down, loosen the soil by running a knife around the edge of the pot, then carefully lift out the root ball. If the plant was properly potted and the soil has been well moistened, the root ball should come out as one solid mass rather than falling to pieces. If you are greeted by a dense network of white, healthy, intertwined roots, it's time to repot.

No matter how desperately your plant needs repotting, you should put it in a container only one size — two inches — larger. Nowadays you can find pots of all shapes, so you might decide on one in a totally different style, say a square pot for a plant that was previously in a round container. It's fine to be daring as long as the new container isn't more than two inches larger than the original. Clay pots are aesthetically more pleasing than plastic containers, and because they are porous, they allow the roots to breathe, thus promoting healthier root growth. However, clay pots are heavier, require more frequent watering, and are more expensive. You may decide that it is worthwhile to spend the extra time and money for clay, since your garden is always on display for family and friends.

All sorts of potting mediums are available for houseplants, but for the best results look for mixes that have a soil base rather than being totally soilless; in other words, they contain sterilized compost, which provides the plant with natural fertilizer and maintains deep green, healthy growth. Plants grown in soilless mixes tend to look pale and chemical-fed, as if they've been nourished solely on a steady diet of fast food.

When you repot, first sprinkle an inch or so of soil on the bottom of the new container. Then place the root ball on top with the soil surface at least a half inch to an inch from the top of the rim (depending upon the size of the container and how much water you suspect it will be needing), center the plant, and fill in around the edges with soil. Tamp the soil down as you work, making certain that no gaps remain. Finally, when you've finished, water the plant and place it in a spot out of direct sun for a few days while the roots recover from the shock of repotting.

Although it's tempting to repot into a generous container to avoid having to repot again in the near future, plants actually prefer to be graduated only one pot size at a time.

Plants That Need to be Pot-bound to Flower

Brugmansia, angel's trumpet
Brunfelsia, yesterday-today-and-tomorrow
Clivia

Impatiens, patient Lucy
Pelargonium, geranium
Solanum, royal robe

FERTILIZING

Potted plants need nourishment, especially when they are growing by leaps and bounds, as is usually the case during the long days of spring and summer. So your fertilizing efforts should be focused primarily on the period from March through November. Through the winter, when light levels are low, extra nutrients are not needed. Even under artificial lights, plants tend to follow their natural growth cycle, resting during the winter and growing more vigorously in spring and summer. Reduce the amount of plant food during the winter, for too much fertilizer can be unhealthy for plants that are trying to rest.

As the light level increases in spring, your plants will become hungry. In summer, houseplants require food once a month. In the brighter environment of a greenhouse, conservatory, sun porch, or sunny, south-facing window, plants may require fertilizing once every three weeks. Heat is also a factor: warmth encourages rampant growth and increases a plant's appetite. On the other hand, in the cool temperatures of a breezeway or unheated sun porch, overfed plants may quickly show symptoms of fertilizer toxicity — yellow veins and mottled leaves.

A newly repotted plant will get all the nourishment it needs from the soil for several months following its graduation into a larger container. However, you should check the foliage for indications of hunger, for some soil mixes provide very little nourishment. On a hungry plant the newest leaves will be pale. However, the color of the leaves is the only problem that should be fixed with a shot of fertilizer. Never feed a plant to remedy wilting or other signs of debilitation.

In general, it's wise to fertilize cautiously rather than overfeed. Never apply plant food in a more concentrated dose than the package directions recommend. Always start with a weak solution, then work up to the full recommended strength after a few applications. Instead of choosing a blossom booster, use a balanced fertilizer such as a 20-20-20, which provides equal parts of nitrogen, phosphorus, and potassium, to encourage healthy growth overall.

PRUNING AND GROOMING

When plants are happy and healthy, they grow vigorously. Plants that grow from the base, such as rex begonias, rhizomatous begonias, sansevieria, spathiphyllum, clivia, and anthurium, may require occasional division, but they don't need to be

The blossoms of some tidy plants drop after they have faded, but many do not.
Flowers that cling after fading should be removed before they court problems.

pruned. Plants that grow from the ends of the stems, however, will often shoot straight toward the ceiling unless steps are taken to curtail their steady upward thrust. Most upright indoor plants require frequent pinching to encourage side shoots and keep the foliage within bounds.

Shaping plants is an important creative skill that is not practiced as often as it should be. Pinching and pruning your container-grown plants will turn them into balanced, well-contoured specimens. When you walk into a house and find a group of handsome, many-branched plants, you know that the resident gardener has invested some thought and effort in pruning.

Houseplants should be pruned early in their careers. Snipping the stem when a plant is only 6 inches tall will encourage branching close to the base, giving it a strong structure on which to expand. Don't let a plant grow up tall and spindly before cutting it back. Although pruning may delay flowering for a few weeks, you'll eventually enjoy more buds as a result of your foresight. And the blossoms will be supported on a symmetrical, balanced framework. If you want your indoor garden to have the lush profusion we associate with an outdoor landscape, pruning will make it happen.

You cannot prune a plant once and consider the job done. You've got to continually encourage branching and maintain symmetry by rotating the plant and clipping all of the stems. Pruning shapes the plant and keeps it tidy. Yellowing or dead leaves should be removed, and spent flowers should be whisked immediately from the scene. Whenever you water, take a moment to deadhead faded flowers and prune off any leaf or branch that isn't enhancing the plant's overall beauty. A properly groomed plant will not be as susceptible to problems as a neglected specimen. Grooming is good preventive medicine.

PESTS AND DISEASES

Where you have plants, you are bound to attract insects. They are a nuisance, but they come with the territory. The most effective means of combating insects is to water your plants properly, fertilize them lightly but regularly, and remove spent leaves and flowers. Weakened plants are easy prey to pests. Even in the plant world the fittest specimens are the most likely to survive. Cool nighttime temperatures help guard against problems, for pests proliferate in a warm environment. Check your plants regularly for signs of insect damage.

When you see a possible pest problem, you should take action promptly. But there's no need to rush out to buy the strongest, meanest chemical on the market. The most common pests of houseplants are whitefly, red spider mites, aphids, and mealybugs, which can be controlled with relatively nontoxic insecticides. An excellent reference dealing specifically with integrated pest management (IPM) is the *Encyclopedia of Natural Insect and Disease Control* by Roger B. Yepsen, Jr., published by Rodale Press. Whitefly can be combated by hanging yellow sticky traps or applying Naturalis O. Red spider mites prefer dry conditions and will vacate the premises if the foliage on which they've been thriving is sprayed with a shot of cold water. Aphids can be dispatched with insecticidal soaps or horticultural oils. Foliar mealybugs can be killed by moistening a cotton swab with rubbing alcohol and applying it to their soft bodies. Before doing battle against a bug, check the label of the insecticide to ascertain if it will control the pest in question. And spray the plant several times at three- to five-day intervals to eradicate further generations. Spray all the nooks and crannies of a plant, penetrating the leaf axils and targeting both the tops and undersides of the leaves. If possible, spray your houseplants outdoors — even insecticidal soap shouldn't be inhaled in close quarters. Then keep the newly sprayed plant out of reach of children and pets. Keep an eye peeled for future infestations.

By being vigilant you can also keep your indoor garden free of disease. A clean environment is the best preventive measure against the diseases that afflict houseplants. Good air circulation, helped by opening a nearby window or placing a fan in the vicinity if necessary, is essential to maintaining the health of your indoor garden. If a plant looks sick, segregate it immediately to keep the problem from spreading. In summer, put the offending plant outside on a porch or balcony. But don't panic, and don't automatically toss the plant out. The symptoms that you see might not be due to disease; your plant may simply be suffering from a change in season or in growing conditions. When the furnace goes on in autumn, houseplants are quite likely to slip into a temporary slump.

If you are in doubt about the identity of and remedy for a disease, seek the advice of your county extension agent. Most states have a staff member of the Department of Agriculture who is versed in the pests and problems of greenhouse and indoor plants. Call your state university to learn how to take advantage of the knowledge and experience of the extension agent. Or call a local public botanical garden that has a collection of indoor-grown tropical plants.

CHAPTER 5:

HOSTING PLANTS INDOORS

Beyond the nuts and bolts of watering, feeding, and defending your house-plants from pests, there are other practical points to consider when you set up an indoor garden. What sorts of containers should you choose? What will they sit on? How can you keep the floor free of the spills that are inevitable when you are toting a full watering can? What do you need to do to ensure that your plants will fit easily into your family's living patterns? Think on a practical level, but find the handsomest solution possible. Look for out-of-the-way places that might be enlivened with plants, then display them with creative flair. A carefully planned, artistically designed indoor garden is a beautiful sight.

FITTING PLANTS INTO YOUR HOME

The first and foremost consideration is the space you plan to fill with plants. How are the windows positioned and how large are they? Do you want to flaunt

Anything — even a teapot — can be enlisted as a cachepot. This creeping fig will survive in low-light areas where other plants may fail.

dramatic, statuesque plants that will wow your friends and neighbors but may block the view or the sun coming into the room? Or do you prefer smaller pots with low-growing plants that leave most of the incoming light unobstructed? Before you go shopping for houseplants, consider where they will live. Think of placements that will show them off, but remember that you will be living with these plants on a rather intimate basis. You don't want them to block passages of frequent traffic flow or obstruct easy access to a curtain rod. No matter how handsome they look, no matter how proud you are of their blossoms, plants need to stay out from underfoot if they are to remain welcome in your household.

When you've decided on the most promising areas of your home from the point of view of family convenience, assess the environmental conditions. Observe the potential growing area over a period of a few weeks before putting your plants there. Notice how the light moves during the day and position your plants to take advantage of it. You may be surprised to find that the sun never reaches one corner of a west-facing windowsill during certain seasons, a salient detail when you're placing your plants. Note the locations of heating vents and air conditioners, and keep plants away from the air flows of those systems.

Fresh air, of course, is very beneficial to plant life. As well as furnishing light,

An intriguing container can make even the most modest plants shine, such as these tiny erodiums grown in a thumb pot and a miniature window box.

Bright-colored pots enliven a collection of cacti and succulents.

windows are also a source of ventilation. In spring and summer, the breeze from an open window helps keep plants free of disease. In all but the coldest part of the year, most plants don't object to a slight draft. However, frigid winter air leaking from a loose window can chill sensitive tropicals such as begonias. Try tucking a little insulation into the crack; that may make all the difference for a cold-sensitive plant.

There are other environmental factors to consider. Kitchens are often brightly lit, and cooking adds humidity to the air, so these are wonderful rooms for most plants. However, if you use gas for cooking, some plants, such as bougainvilleas, begonias, and hibiscus, may drop their leaves. Similarly, gas faux-fireplaces can leak fumes that are not perceptible or dangerous to you but can be hazardous to some plants. This doesn't mean that you cannot grow houseplants, for not all are sensitive to gas fumes. Just be aware of the problem and seek out plants that won't mind the situation.

WHERE WILL YOUR PLANTS SINK THEIR ROOTS?

Many factors come into play when choosing the containers that hold the plant's prime sources of nourishment — soil, oxygen, and water. Just as each plant has particular traits in its leaves, stems, and growth habit, each one has different root characteristics as well. It's important to make a good match between pot shape and root structure. Certain plants, such as roses and rosemaries, send their roots plunging straight down, and they are well suited to the deep, lean pots that are sometimes known as rose pots or long Toms. Begonias and geraniums, on the other hand, send their roots wandering horizontally. They prefer the squat, wide containers known as azalea pots. Creeping ground covers, such as selaginella, peperomia, laurentia, and lysimachia, tend to be anchored with short roots and prefer shallow containers with wide mouths. Vines usually need plenty of ballast to support their upward growth; they prefer heavy, deep containers with a broad footprint. Choose a pot that you find appealing, but make certain it is practical as well.

Consider what a pot is made of as well as its shape. Unfortunately, for reasons that are purely economic, houseplants are usually sold in rather ugly leprechaun green plastic containers. Plastic is inexpensive, which may explain why retailers have wholeheartedly embraced it for potting purposes. However, on your home windowsill, clay might look more pleasing. From an aesthetic perspective, the earth tone of terra cotta splendidly complements the subtle green hues of

Plants for Deep Pots

Bougainvillea	Heliotrope
Brugmansia, angel's trumpet	Hibiscus
Camellia	*Laurus,* sweet bay
Citrus	*Osteospermum,* Ecklonis daisy
Clerodendrum, glory-bower	*Passiflora,* passionflower
Clivia	Rosemary
Gardenia	*Zygocactus,* Thanksgiving cactus

Spring-blooming primroses lend themselves to rustic baskets. With a plastic liner, you can plant directly in the basket or tuck the pot inside.

Plants for Shallow Pots

Begonias

Calathea

Calceolaria, pocketbook plant

Cineraria

Cissus, kangaroo vine

Forced bulbs

Fuchsia

Jasmine

Mandevilla

Maranta, prayer plant

Narcissus, paper-whites

Ocimum, sweet basil

Phalaenopsis, moth orchid

Plectranthus, Swedish ivy

Violet, pansy

Foliage plants for a north-facing window have extra panache in containers that echo the greens in the leaves.

plant foliage. On a practical level, clay breathes freely, giving the roots access to oxygen. Thus, in many cases, plants in clay containers tend to be healthier and more robust. However, clay is porous. So plants grown in clay pots will dry out more quickly than those in plastic. That's not a problem for the plant, but it might be inconvenient for your schedule. If you travel often, or if your houseplants are dwelling at a weekend cottage, plastic pots may be preferable. But there's no reason why you can't hide a plastic pot within a more pleasing ornamental container. Looks are important when you're living with a plant.

Pots made of other materials are also available. Although cement is heavy, if your houseplants aren't going to be moved around a lot, this can be a very handsome option. In fact, the latest fashion is cement containers embedded with pottery shards. Or, if you do like to move your plants frequently, try fiberglass containers that are made to look like cement. They aren't nearly so heavy and

Imaginative pots and woven cachepots enhance the flower colors and add to the festivity of blooming holiday plants.

look so similar to it that even the most discerning gardeners will be fooled. There's only one word of caution: make certain your fiberglass container is furnished with drainage holes.

Forced bulbs, pansies, and other houseplants that take center stage for only a few months can dwell in woven baskets fitted with plastic liners. Many baskets sold in garden centers come equipped with a liner specifically for that purpose. But if you have a favorite basket that has no protection, simply mold a plastic bag around the inside before potting. It will work fine temporarily — and houseplant displays need not last forever. There's nothing wrong with filling your home with fleeting pansies in baskets to keep you entertained between Easter and the last frost date in your area, when you can put them outside in the garden.

All sorts of found objects can be used as containers or cachepots. You can find genuine Victorian cachepots (ornamental glazed pots into which the actual

Creeping fig, wandering Jew, and ivy are striking in an indoor strawberry pot. Be sure to rotate the pot regularly and carefully water all the little balconies.

pot is slipped) in antique shops. But there's no need to invest in antiques. Use your imagination: mixing bowls, old buckets, and chamber pots make wonderful cachepots. Florists have learned to adapt all sorts of odd objects for use as vases. Anything that will hold soil can hold a houseplant for at least a short period of time.

Saucers or drip trays are an important element of any successful window garden. Plants wear out their welcome rapidly if you are continually mopping up puddles from the floor. If your plant sits on furniture or on a wooden floor, make certain that its saucer is glazed to prevent leakage. Nowadays, you can find glazed and crackle-finished saucers that are just as ornamental as the pots they drain. The copper or plastic drip trays lined with pebbles that are used to increase humidity are also handy for collecting excess water. You'll need to provide further protection if your plants sit on valuable pieces of furniture; a cork coaster

A formal room requires a sophisticated selection of plants. Aspidistra, croton, and zebra plant, combined here with seasonal blooming hyacinths, create a sedate mood.

under the saucer will help keep mildew from forming on the surface underneath. The Victorians tucked lace doilies beneath houseplants to soak up spills, and you can buy intricate hand-crocheted antique doilies for a song nowadays. Even with protection, though, it's never wise to place a plant on a piano. Although you may be the most graceful human being on the planet, accidents can happen.

WHERE YOUR PLANTS WILL SIT

Many people adopt a houseplant without visualizing where that new member of the family will live when it arrives home. The most obvious solution is the windowsill. If your windowsill isn't wide enough for houseplants, you can purchase extenders that clip on underneath the window and rest on brackets. The trick is to find one that doesn't tilt when you place heavy pots on it. Not only does a slanted surface carry the potential danger of sending potted plants crashing to their doom, but water will dribble over their rims on the lower side, which means that the plant never gets a thorough soaking. Select a sill extender that has strong support beneath it to carry the weight of a clay pot and its contents. You can also find clear plastic shelves that fit directly on the windowpanes via suction cups. The clear plastic blends with the window glass and disappears from sight, so the plant seems to be suspended in thin air. These shelves are great as long as you select a reliable model. Disaster can easily strike if the weight of the pots exceeds the strength of the suctioning unit. And keep in mind that plants gain weight when you water them.

If you have sliding glass doors or glass French doors, you can simply set your plants right on the floor. Cluster them together, surrounding the large plants with an adoring brood of smaller ones of various sizes, shapes, and leaf textures. If you compose the setting thoughtfully and use plants that spill over their container edges, it will look as if a garden is growing out of the floor. And when your garden is set safely on the ground, you needn't worry about the heft of each container — even a 14-inch pot can dwell comfortably on the floor.

If windowsills or the floor aren't options, your plants will need some sort of shelf, table, or stand near a window to get the benefit of incoming sunbeams. All sorts of stands can be used — you needn't select one that is specifically constructed to hold plants. Tables are wide enough to allow you to group plants with matching foliage and flowers. An old Formica or enamel kitchen table is particularly convenient if you tend to spill when you water or if you allow your toddler to try her hand at watering the houseplants. Antique dry sinks and potting benches also work well. Or purchase an old table at a yard sale or flea market. It doesn't need to be beautiful — the surface will soon be covered with plants anyway.

There are many types of plant stands on the market, ranging from pared-down, Shaker-style wooden versions with long legs and small tops to tile-topped stands with slender metal legs, which are appropriate both indoors and outside. You can use a round-topped Victorian reading table with curvaceous turned legs, or you can upend a wooden shipping crate and press it into service. Any piece of furniture, including filing cabinets, dressers, and bedside tables, can be employed as long as they provide a level surface and stand at the proper height, about flush with the windowsill. It's not necessary for the pot itself to bask in the sun. In fact, during the heat of the summer, it's preferable to shelter roots from baking sun. Australian plants are particularly sensitive; leptospermum, prostanthera, and grevillea prefer cool, shaded roots.

Old wooden ironing boards make wonderful plant shelves, and they're easy to find at flea markets. Nineteenth-century ironing boards were much wider than

Any shelf can hold an array of plants, but this plant stand was custom made for the purpose, and it neatly hides the tray on which the potted alpines sit.

those we use today, making them perfect for grouping an array of potted plants. They adjust to several different heights, so you can bring the top flush with your window edge. You can also use benches from picnic tables, old bleachers, or step stools. Wooden steamer trunks and blanket chests are good surfaces for house-plants. To vary the height of your pots and ensure that plants are not sitting in one another's shadows, place them on blocks of wood or small pedestals. All sorts

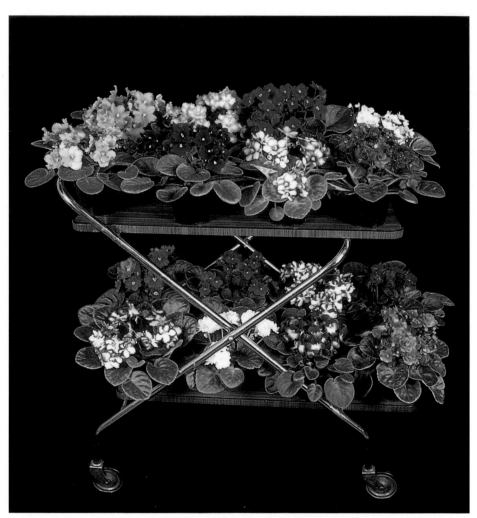

African violets look best en masse, and this two-tiered serving cart makes a great display area.

of acanthus-leaved columns are sold for this purpose, but not all are waterproof and will have to be protected.

You can combine several heights of shelves and plant stands for a multilevel display. Just as you mix textures of foliage, you can also juxtapose different types of stands. Or purchase a wedding cake–style plant rack. Stepladders are wonderful for displaying plants, for several pots can fit on each rung of the ladder. Shop-display étagères are available in many shapes, including useful quarter- and half-round units that fit perfectly into corners. Some are wood, but many are made with slatted metal shelves, providing plenty of air circulation and allowing light to penetrate from all angles.

FINDING NOOKS AND CRANNIES FOR HOUSEPLANTS

Walk through your home and evaluate all the spaces you might be able to use for plants. A clutter-accumulating corner or out-of-the-way sideboard may be begging to be converted into a horticultural haven. If you have a closet that happens to be in a sunny spot, why waste good light on ice skates and tennis rackets? And most closets have shelves just waiting to hold houseplants. Take off the closet door, add artificial plant lights if necessary, and change the space from storage to display.

Unused rooms can become secret gardens. Breezeways, mud rooms, and unheated porches can hold plants during all but the coldest seasons of the year. Make plants a top priority, and you'll be surprised at the spaces that step out of the woodwork. And if you're inventive, you may find that you already have all the stands and display shelves you need without having to invest a penny in your new project.

CHAPTER 6:

FANCY FOOTWORK WITH HOUSEPLANTS

There are many clever touches that can make your indoor garden more exciting and unique. By lining your sill with window boxes, you can turn common houseplants such as chrysanthemums or poinsettias into a spectacular display. A trellis can turn a modest vine into a showpiece. If you've found a plant whose branches cascade down, show off that trait to its best advantage by exhibiting it on a stand that accentuates its long, flowing lines. You want your indoor garden to do more than merely survive — you want to create an exceptional and dramatic display.

WINDOW BOXES INDOORS

Placing window boxes indoors is not a novel idea. In fact, the first such boxes, meant to be small indoor gardens to be enjoyed when the landscape outside was

Provided with an imaginative support, ivy will make a topiary almost overnight. Passionflowers also quickly become living sculpture.

Grouped together so that the colors harmonize, and with pots hidden behind a cornice, the spring garden seems to be growing happily indoors.

sleeping, were set up on the inside sill of the window. And window boxes remain a wonderful way to display a grouping of houseplants. Most garden centers now offer 12- or 14-inch-long boxes that are the perfect size for indoor gardening. Often sold as herb boxes, they work well for most houseplants, as long as those you're planning to box won't outgrow their constricted containers.

Consider yourself fortunate if your sill is broad enough to hold a narrow box. If not, you can set your box on a plant stand or place it on a stepladder positioned in a sunny spot. Although it may be difficult to find trays made to fit under window boxes, long, slender copper trays can be used to catch the inevitable spills when you water. Or use a cookie-baking tray underneath.

Tucked together in a rustic birch-bark window box and hidden beneath a layer of sheet moss, individual pots of flowering bulbs and primroses can be displayed while the blossoms are fresh, then switched for fresh blooms.

Kept conveniently in the kitchen to flavor whatever happens to be cooking, herbs are commonly grown in window boxes. Parsley, hyssop, marjoram, and mint all work well.

Plants for Indoor Window Boxes

Sunny south-facing windows
Brachycome, Swan River daisy
Browallia
Cacti and succulents
Herbs: parsley, sage, rosemary, thyme, basil, oregano
Myrtus, biblical myrtle
Pelargonium, geranium
Portulaca, moss rose
Verbena

East- or west-facing windows
Impatiens
Fuchsia, especially miniature varieties
Begonias
Streptocarpella
Streptocarpus, Cape primrose
Saintpaulia, African violet

Shady north-facing windows
Cissus, kangaroo vine
Cyperus, umbrella plant
Hedera helix, ivy
Philodendron
Sansevieria, rattlesnake plant
Saxifraga sarmentosa, strawberry begonia
Scilla

When planting a window box indoors, select plants that will grow at approximately the same rate so they don't compete with one another, and leave enough space between the plants so they have room to bush out. Most of the basics that you follow when growing any houseplant also hold true for those in windowsill boxes. But there is one important factor to consider: because your window box receives light from only one direction, you should turn it around once a week to encourage balanced growth and promote bud set on both sides.

The narrow window boxes used indoors are called herb boxes because of the popularity of clustering several edible herbs conveniently together. Not surprisingly, their most common location is a kitchen window sill, where the herbs are easily available to the cook. Many herbs can be grown in an indoor box, including basil (especially the miniature-leaved types), fennel, thyme, rosemary (especially the prostrate form), savory, oregano, parsley, and sage. Clip the contained herbs often to flavor dinner, and they'll remain tidy over a long period of time.

Besides herbs, all sorts of plants are perfect for window boxes. Trailing plants work well because they drape over the sides. Small-leaved plants are easy to keep under control. Experiment with different types, combining those that seem to balance each other in color and size. If a plant exceeds your expectations and outgrows its neighbors, simply dig it out and replace it with something else.

WORKING WITH VINES INDOORS

Vines are some of the handsomest houseplants. They have incredible kinetic energy, and those athletic tendencies can be harnessed to good advantage on a windowsill. Most vines send out rapid-growing, whippy arms and legs groping for a support. Wrap those stems around a trellis or drape them around your window, and you've got instant impact. Few sights can compare with a bougainvillea, for example, laden with sprays of sweet-pealike blossoms, twining gracefully around a window frame. A thoughtfully wrapped vine winding around its support is a living sculpture. Each stem may not be heavily laden with leaves, for vines often have lengthy spaces between leaves, but the plant makes its splash with the splendor of intertwining greenery. And flowers aren't essential to the drama: a creatively twined cissus, ivy, or muehlenbeckia can be just as riveting as a vine smothered in bloom. The beauty of a vine is its growth habit.

Flowers are an important bonus, of course. A flowering thunbergia, bougainvillea, asarina, jasmine, gelsemium, or mandevilla can be incredibly beautiful. Blossoming vines speak more eloquently than many upright plants because the winding action of the branches clusters their flowers together. A florist could not possibly compose a more breathtaking arrangement than the design that nature concocts on a vine — and no vase is needed.

Vines contribute an appearance of wildness, as though nature had entered the room unleashed. In truth, however, you want to keep your vines under close surveillance. Passionflower, jasmine, thunbergia, asarina, hoya, and ivy all make splendid houseplants as long as you keep abreast of their progress. Nothing looks worse than a wayward vine sending straggly growth hither and yon in an undisciplined fashion.

Vines require a little extra care. The first step is to select an appropriate support; the type depends upon the kind of vine you're bracing. A vine travels in one of four ways. Either it gropes by tendrils (this is how members of the pea family become upwardly mobile), or it attaches itself by sucker roots (as ivy and creeping fig do), or it leans (allamanda and bougainvillea are leaners), or it winds around its support (as thunbergia and asarina travel). The support should suit the vine's mode of movement. Most vines can begin their careers with a single thick bamboo stake, but the majority will quickly outgrow that initial brace. The earlier you provide an appropriate support that can handle the plant's future growth habit, the better.

Vines

Allamanda, golden trumpet
Aristolochia, Dutchman's pipe
Bougainvillea
Clerodendrum, glory-bower
Gelsemium, Carolina jasmine
Hardenbergia, happy wanderer
Jasmine
Mandevilla
Passionflower
Solanum, royal robe
Thunbergia, black-eyed Susan
Trachelospermum, Confederate
 jasmine

To shore up a leaner, find a large and sturdy structure with crosspieces capable of bearing the vine's weight. A 3-foot-wide rose trellis would be perfect. Rather than using wood, you might look for an iron trellis that won't deteriorate when the vine reaches maturity. Featherweight vines that twine with tendrils, such as cissus and passionflower, can be encouraged to camouflage a tepee-shaped trellis made of wire or twigs. The components should be slender enough for the tendrils to easily ensnare. An Eiffel Tower–shaped trellis is ideal, especially if it is 3 feet tall or more. Ivy and other vines that adhere to their support with sucker

A whippy vine such as winter-blooming jasmine can become an instant wreath simply by winding the stems around a wire frame.

The wayward stems of miniature cissus can be persuaded to climb whatever support is at hand.

You can harness the kangaroo vine's athletic energy to good advantage by potting a few cuttings in a planter and letting the tendrils climb up a frame. Within no time the plant will become a masterpiece (left). Allowed to roam over a twig frame, smilax quickly camouflages its support (above).

roots can be given moss or some other flat surface to cover. Be wary when you work with these vines — those roots can adhere to plaster and other surfaces where they're not welcome.

Small winding climbers such as asarina and muehlenbeckia (also known as the maidenhair vine) can be successfully trained on wreath- or sphere-shaped frames made of wire no thicker than clothes hangers. Sections of fencing or even bird cages can provide a structure to which climbers can cling. All kinds of supports and trellises are on the market; you can find truly handsome treillage and wirework both fanciful and elegant, both handmade and factory produced. Look for sturdy welded metal units made of heavy wire with many-pronged feet that can sink several inches into the soil. When supporting a hefty vine, the buried base is just as important as the upper framework.

Although passionflower is quite savvy about linking with its support the moment it's provided, most vines need a few lessons to help them reach upward. Guidance should be given before a vine goes off in the wrong direction. If you have to wrench tendrils free from the curtain rod or some other equally inappropriate foothold, they are likely to die back, and buds may drop due to the shock. Tender young growth is often damaged when you try to wrestle it free from an unintended support. To avoid this difficulty, start guiding your vine in the right direction early on.

When you're training a vine, tie the stems in place loosely with pipe cleaners or raffia, which won't girdle them. Guide the vine in a spiral path, then continue to weave it into its support wherever you want it to travel. Vines need pruning to encourage side branches and fullness, and they can choke themselves out if they aren't thinned occasionally. To prolong a vine's life and encourage fresh growth, prune back stems that are tired and sparse nearly to the base. Heavy pruning will give a vine new life.

Repotting becomes cumbersome once a vine has begun to twine around its support, so start it off in a generous pot. And when an energetic vine is making rapid growth, fertilize it frequently. Don't overdo it, mind you — like any other plant, a vine can suffer from fertilizer toxicity. But watch out for signs of hunger such as paling foliage. Also, since they're supporting a bounty of foliage, vines dry out more often than upright plants, so make sure they don't wilt. Bougainvilleas are particularly dramatic when signaling that they desire a drink. Keep them evenly watered, but don't overreact; bougainvilleas actually bloom better after they've wilted once or twice.

Insects can be a problem when a vine becomes dense. Keep a vigilant eye out for signs of bugs. And penetrate deep within the inner growth when you spray for insects. They love to lodge in nooks and crannies that are difficult to reach with insecticides.

HANGING PLANTS

Rather than climbing, some plants prefer to dangle. The traditional method of displaying a hanging plant is to nail up a bracket somewhere near a window and suspend the plant from there. This certainly works, and it's pleasing to the eye if you can find a basket that is more attractive than the typical plastic types, which tend to be stark white or leprechaun green. Eventually, if all goes well, the plastic hanging pot will be entirely camouflaged by the cascading plant. But in the meantime, the plastic pot always seems to stare you straight in the eye. Any alternative is an improvement.

With the help of a clip-on heavy-gauge wire hanger (readily available in several lengths from greenhouse supply companies or garden centers), any clay pot can be displayed aloft. When you're working with a heavy hanging pot, it's wise to fill it with a light, peat-based potting soil. Or you can purchase a hand-thrown clay hanging pot. There are many other possibilities. The lightest-weight option is a woven basket with a plastic liner. Even a half coconut shell can be enlisted. Steer away from wire baskets filled with long-fiber moss, though. It's true that they provide plenty of oxygen to the roots, but the moss always sheds and water dribbles out whenever you try to quench the plant's thirst. Speaking of which, watering is a major issue with hanging plants. Plants aloft dry out twice as often as their earth-bound counterparts. Hanging pots should always be equipped with a device to catch excess water. Most plastic and hand-thrown clay pots have drip trays conveniently attached. Or you can hide an ordinary pot within a hanging cachepot that is glazed inside to prevent leakage.

Hanging Plants

Abutilon, flowering maple
Cissus, kangaroo vine
Diascia, twinspurs
Fuchsia
Gynura, purple passion plant
Hedera helix, ivy
Hermannia, honeybells
Heterocentron, Spanish shawl
Kalanchoe
Pilea, cat's tongue plant
Scaevola, fan flower
Peperomia

With only four cuttings nestled together in a hanging container, Kalanchoe pumila
fills out to blossom in midwinter.

Hanging plants make a dramatic statement, but they do monopolize a large
chunk of space and they may reduce your incoming light dramatically. However,
a fully clothed hanging plant can serve the same purpose as a curtain — obstructing the view into your home at night and filtering the sun during the day.

There are many other ways to display hanging plants. You can grow one in
a tall pot, pedestal pot, or long Tom and simply drape the limp stems over the
edges of a slender plant stand or encourage the stems to dangle over the edge of
a table.

However you display it, a hanging plant needs to be groomed and pruned
meticulously. Pot three or four cuttings (it's best to start with young, trainable

plants) in a triangular or diamond configuration to encourage symmetrical growth. Then pinch the fledglings frequently to make them branch out and gain fullness — most hanging plants are not self-branching. The initial pruning is essential, but later discipline is also necessary. The moment a hanging plant begins to get straggly, prune the stems back. You will forfeit flowers temporarily, but you will be rewarded with a more ambitious blossom show later.

TOPIARY

Instead of working with the traits that Mother Nature built into your plant, you can persuade it to follow your whim. Coax an ivy into a heart shape or cover a replica of the Statue of Liberty in creeping fig. There's no limit to what you can do.

Some topiary tricks can be accomplished quite easily, without an advanced degree in horticulture. Many pliable-stemmed plants, such as rosemary, myrtle, coprosma, fuchsia, and serissa, can be encouraged to wind around a wreath frame or wire hoop. You'll find the heavy-gauge wire frames available at many garden centers and craft shops. Creating a living wreath isn't a difficult feat, but it does require a little extra attention and care. When you're shaping nonvining plants with rigid stems to a frame, it's essential to start with young specimens and begin training early. Plant two cuttings in the container and gently bend each to follow the lines of the frame, securing it with pipe cleaners every few inches. If possible, wind the stem around the wire to give it a firmer grasp and camouflage the support. As the plants fill in, keep the side shoots clipped to encourage branching. A popular variation on the living-wreath theme, especially for Valentine's Day, is to substitute a heart-shaped frame for the round one.

Wreaths and one-dimensional shapes are a simple form of topiary, but the art can become more complex. You can mold plants into double orbs, pyramids, and all sorts of geometric shapes by wrapping the stems around the frame as the plant grows. You can experiment with running different types of plants on separate arms of a frame. You can weave together ivies with diverse leaf shapes or

> ## *Plants for Topiary*
>
> Coprosma
> Creeping fig
> *Gelsemium,* Carolina jasmine
> *Hedera helix,* ivy
> Rosemary

With only four cuttings nestled together in a hanging container, Kalanchoe pumila
fills out to blossom in midwinter.

Hanging plants make a dramatic statement, but they do monopolize a large
chunk of space and they may reduce your incoming light dramatically. However,
a fully clothed hanging plant can serve the same purpose as a curtain — obstructing the view into your home at night and filtering the sun during the day.

There are many other ways to display hanging plants. You can grow one in
a tall pot, pedestal pot, or long Tom and simply drape the limp stems over the
edges of a slender plant stand or encourage the stems to dangle over the edge of
a table.

However you display it, a hanging plant needs to be groomed and pruned
meticulously. Pot three or four cuttings (it's best to start with young, trainable

plants) in a triangular or diamond configuration to encourage symmetrical growth. Then pinch the fledglings frequently to make them branch out and gain fullness — most hanging plants are not self-branching. The initial pruning is essential, but later discipline is also necessary. The moment a hanging plant begins to get straggly, prune the stems back. You will forfeit flowers temporarily, but you will be rewarded with a more ambitious blossom show later.

TOPIARY

Instead of working with the traits that Mother Nature built into your plant, you can persuade it to follow your whim. Coax an ivy into a heart shape or cover a replica of the Statue of Liberty in creeping fig. There's no limit to what you can do.

Some topiary tricks can be accomplished quite easily, without an advanced degree in horticulture. Many pliable-stemmed plants, such as rosemary, myrtle, coprosma, fuchsia, and serissa, can be encouraged to wind around a wreath frame or wire hoop. You'll find the heavy-gauge wire frames available at many garden centers and craft shops. Creating a living wreath isn't a difficult feat, but it does require a little extra attention and care. When you're shaping nonvining plants with rigid stems to a frame, it's essential to start with young specimens and begin training early. Plant two cuttings in the container and gently bend each to follow the lines of the frame, securing it with pipe cleaners every few inches. If possible, wind the stem around the wire to give it a firmer grasp and camouflage the support. As the plants fill in, keep the side shoots clipped to encourage branching. A popular variation on the living-wreath theme, especially for Valentine's Day, is to substitute a heart-shaped frame for the round one.

Wreaths and one-dimensional shapes are a simple form of topiary, but the art can become more complex. You can mold plants into double orbs, pyramids, and all sorts of geometric shapes by wrapping the stems around the frame as the plant grows. You can experiment with running different types of plants on separate arms of a frame. You can weave together ivies with diverse leaf shapes or

---

Plants for Topiary

Coprosma
Creeping fig
Gelsemium, Carolina jasmine
Hedera helix, ivy
Rosemary

experiment with other creative combinations, such as plants with variegated and nonvariegated leaves. The trick is to find plants with similar speeds and habits of growth.

Stuffed topiary is even easier than the one-dimensional forms. Purchase a chicken-wire frame made for this purpose and fill it with dampened sphagnum moss. Then plant cuttings of ground covers such as creeping fig, baby's tears, or ivy directly in the moss. When it is complete, turn the frame every few days to expose all sides to light, and continue to keep the inner moss evenly watered throughout its life. Along with geometric shapes, animal forms such as turtles, cats, monkeys, and rabbits are popular.

Creating a standard is a time-honored, enduring, and fulfilling type of topiary. The art goes back to Roman times and has been practiced on and off ever since. Right now, standards are definitely in vogue. A finished one is worth quite a hefty sum of money, and may become an heirloom. A standard can best be described as a houseplant trained to resemble the lollipop-shaped trees you once drew in kindergarten. It's a ball on a stick.

Standards vary in height from 6 inches to 6 feet. The crown can be as small as 4 inches in diameter or as ambitious as a 3-foot-wide orb. They are usually made of rosemary, myrtle, leptospermum, coprosma, heliotrope, or some other tiny-leaved herb. But most straight-stemmed plants can be coaxed to assume a standard shape. And a round orb is not the only shape that can be balanced on top of the single stem; you can train lantana or fuchsia to become a weeping standard with cascading branches.

Nurseries often make standards by grafting a rose or hibiscus crown onto a

Plants for Standards

Coleus
Fuchsia
Genista, Canary Island broom
Hebe
Heliotrope

Hibiscus
Leptospermum, Australian tea tree
Myrtus, biblical myrtle
Rosemary
Scented geraniums

thick-stemmed rootstock. This is not a task that most amateurs should attempt. It's simpler, though more time-consuming, to make a standard simply by encouraging a single-stemmed plant to grow up arrow straight. Tie the stem to a bamboo stake to keep it in line. As it grows, denude the stem of side branches but leave a tuft of growth on the top. When it reaches the height you want, pinch the top and let the upper side branches grow out to form a crown. All the while, your standard-in-training will need constant rotating to make certain that the stem stays straight and the side branches grow out symmetrically. Continue to prune the side shoots, training the plant into the shape you wish it to assume. A poodle cut, with many balls on the stem, is a further whimsy along the same lines.

OTHER FANCY EFFECTS

You can create a tiny indoor garden with miniature plants and dollhouse-sized gates and arbors. Or you might want to make an Elizabethan knot garden in a pot, using a wide, flat container and planting tiny herbs in intersecting circles and triangles. For a low-maintenance fantasy, plant dozens of different rosette-forming succulents in a flat wreath; it won't require water more than once every two weeks.

For a project that will endure throughout your lifetime and increase your Zen approach to life, try your hand at bonsai. Take a small-leaved plant, confine its roots to a painfully small container, and patiently remove extraneous branches until it looks like a tiny tree with gracefully arched limbs. Deciduous trees and conifers are traditionally enlisted for bonsai. However, they require a period of very cold conditions so they can slip into their dormancy cycle. In fact, old and

Plants for Indoor Bonsai

Camellia	Rosemary
Carissa, Natal plum	Semituberous begonias
Coprosma	*Serissa,* snow rose
Myrtus, biblical myrtle	Chrysanthemum

valuable bonsai are sometimes kept in climatically controlled chambers so the pots don't crack and the roots don't suffer from the freezing and thawing that occurs outdoors. During the winter bonsai must be watered carefully.

If you don't have the proper environment to make a deciduous tree bonsai, use a houseplant that is reminiscent of a tree in miniature, such as a semituberous begonia or a tree-form oxalis. These plants display the proper look but don't require a winter cooling period. However, they will require additional care. Any plant that is crammed into an undersized bonsai pot must be watered more frequently than one grown under less stressful conditions.

Houseplants are infinitely entertaining. Once you've gotten the knack of growing one family of plants, you can try another group. When you've mastered a particular art form, such as topiary, you can experiment with something different. There's so much to do and learn. And houseplants are a hobby that you can enjoy day and night without leaving home.

CHAPTER 7:

DESIGNING WITH HOUSEPLANTS

You can approach your indoor garden from various different angles. You might let it reflect the era of your home. If the prevailing motif is Colonial, herbs and primroses would be appropriate. If your house is a rambling Victorian with bay windows, tropical begonias and ferns would enhance the look of the era. Architectural plants such as sansevierias and succulents complement the clean lines of a modern interior. But there are no hard and fast rules. Choose whatever suits your fancy. When houseplants are potted in appropriate containers and displayed in a manner in keeping with their surroundings, they naturally blend with their scene.

FITTING PLANTS INTO YOUR DECOR

Different spaces in your house suggest different moods. A front parlor often has a formal ambience, making it a good space for grand palms, Boston ferns, or your grandmother's heirloom begonia. Kitchens, pantries, and other work spaces are

Beyond the traditional forced bulbs, primroses and cyclamen provide a harbinger of spring and a riot of color before the season actually arrives.

A monochromatic palette can be just as eloquent as a combination of many colors.
This row of 'Tête-à-tête' and 'Jumblie' narcissus is extremely expressive.

not nearly as serious. A casual grouping of useful herbs to clip for cooking looks very comfortable in the kitchen. Potted pansies and cyclamens are perfect for a breezeway that acts as a bridge between the landscape outdoors and the garden inside. Make certain that the space receives filtered light rather than full sun and that the temperature in the entryway remains cool.

Mood is important, but it's imperative to consider the growing environment. In deciding whether to grow herbs beside the kitchen stove, remember that herbs will tolerate a dry atmosphere but usually prefer a cool location. Flowering plants need a sunny spot to set buds, and tropicals need warm, humid conditions to thrive. If you enjoy playing with varieties of fancy foliage, then a shady window will suffice. Or try positioning flowering plants close to a window and scattering a few ferns or foliage plants in the shade they create. Familiarize yourself with the plants you admire and their needs, then consider the space you plan to fill. Your goal should be a happy marriage between plants and place.

BRINGING THE OUTDOORS INTO YOUR HOME

Think of your indoor growing area as a garden. The same design theories that you follow when laying out a backyard garden also hold true on the windowsill. The most successful gardens both outdoors and inside feature a combination of different leaf shapes, sizes, textures, and patterns. Diversity is essential, and houseplants offer plenty of variability.

Just as you work to enhance the color scheme in the garden outdoors, you can do the same in your house. An entire windowsill populated by orange-flowering abutilons might be tedious, but if you choose abutilons in several different shades, the display will be an interesting one. A windowsill filled with begonias, pansies, African violets, or whatever suits your fancy will be most impressive if you vary the flower color. Or you can mix and match several different kinds of plants to create a gardenesque scene.

Use plants as focal points. Put an agave with long, pointed leaves into an urn, then arrange smaller cacti and succulents around its pedestal. Clip a pair of rosemaries into tall standards and set them on either side of a window lined with less dramatic culinary herbs. Dangle a plectranthus from the center of the curtain rod and face the windowsill with a display of cascading plants. Let your windowsill make a strong statement.

A MOVABLE FEAST

Unlike most elements of your home decor, an indoor garden is always in flux. Except for replacing a rug that has faded over the years or a couch that has become slightly threadbare, most people don't alter their furnishings drastically. But the scene on your windowsill can be transformed as often as you want. Your indoor garden will also change with time and maturity. You might have begun by selecting an assortment of little plants that fit your color scheme or that you found fascinating. But over time some plants move on and others replace them. When the fern sends fronds swooping down and the aralia dons its mature foliage, you may need to find different places to display those plants to best advantage.

When it becomes necessary to reshuffle your plants, you'll find that a potted garden is delightfully mobile; even the most cumbersome container can be fitted with a wheel caddy. And mistakes in size or placement are easily repaired. Designing a window garden is not like planting a maple grove. You can be daring without suffering consequences, for no display has to be permanent on the windowsill.

In the garden, after the daffodils have come and gone, you can't cut the tired foliage until it dies down, but indoors you have more freedom. When a houseplant stops blossoming or slips into dormancy, there's no reason why it must remain in a prime location. Banish the slumbering clivia to a back room and put another flowering plant in its place. After their moment of glory is past, former bloomers can be recycled. There's no reason to keep that tired-looking poinsettia for an entire year waiting for next December's holidays. Even if you bring it back into bloom, it will never look as good as a new one. Donate those seasonal performers that are readily available at any supermarket to the compost pile or garbage can.

THEME WINDOWSILLS

Theme gardens, such as children's gardens, scented gardens, white-flowering gardens, and so on, are definitely in vogue outdoors, and they're equally effective inside. In fact, when a garden is at your elbow, its theme becomes more meaningful; the leaves and flowers beside your favorite easy chair are more readily enjoyed. And on the warmer side of the windowpanes you can create themes that are difficult or impossible to orchestrate outside, such as a garden of Australian winter bloomers.

Color Themes. Of course, you will want to use leaf and flower colors indoors that are compatible with your decor. All aspects of your home should be in harmony in both mood and palette. And you may choose to avoid certain colors for reasons of preference. Some folks don't like magenta, others shy away from orange — it's a personal thing. On the other hand, if you're fond of particular hues, you may want to devote a windowsill entirely to plants that display those colors in their leaves or flowers.

Back at the beginning of the century, blue gardens outdoors were all the rage. One reason for their popularity was the challenge of finding blue-flowering

When the ground is still frozen outdoors, the intense colors of spring bulbs in an assortment of containers provide a welcome note.

Blue-Flowering Houseplants

Brunfelsia australis, yesterday-today-and-tomorrow

Clerodendrum ugandense, blue butterfly flower

Evolvulus, blue daze

Felicia amelloides, kingfisher daisy

Hebe 'Amy'

Heliotrope

Otacanthus caeruleus, Brazilian snapdragon

Pentas 'California Lavender', Egyptian stars

Plectranthus hilliardiae

Thunbergia grandiflora, blue trumpet vine

Verbena 'Homestead Blue'

plants. To feed the demand, hybridizers worked to add blues to plant varieties that hadn't included those shades in their color range. And collectors brought plants with blue blossoms back from the tropics and introduced them into common cultivation. Nowadays you can readily find blue-blossoming plants for your home in all shapes and sizes.

Blue is just one example; you might be daring and make a magenta indoor garden of bougainvillea, fuchsia, Spanish shawl, and chenille plant. Or you might choose a more subtle theme and work with white and silver. There's no need to confine the collection merely to flowers: look for blue-green leaves and silver foliage to enhance the shades of blossoms.

Keep in mind that incandescent lights and fluorescent tubes alter the colors of blossoms. Blues may appear pink under artificial light, and reds can also change hue. The intensity of the light also affects color. Flowers and leaves often fail to show off their true colors under low light.

Scented Gardens. Scented flowers and aromatic leaves truly come into their own indoors. When plants sit close at hand, you can sample their fragrant wares frequently. And if several scented bloomers are nestled together, the aromas blend into a wonderful perfume. The confined space acts like a corked perfume jar, while the indoor heat draws essential oils from a flower's throat. Citrus, jasmine, trachelospermum, fragrant violet, gardenia, and hoya are all legendary performers, discreetly sending their scents to intermingle with the atmosphere. In midwinter a fragrant indoor garden is heady stuff.

Certain plants are fragrant only after dark, and there's nothing more reward-ing than coming home from a long, hard day's work to a little fragrant night music. When you think about it, the living room is a more appropriate place for night bloomers than the backyard. Trachelospermum and jasmine are more fra-grant after sunset, and angel's trumpet, certain hoyas, and night-blooming jas-mine emit their aromas only in the evening.

Although fragrant flowers delight your nose, they don't usually add a lot of bright color to your home. Most fragrant flowers, including jasmine, angel's

Scented Flowers

Cestrum, night-blooming jasmine
Citrus
Fragrant violet
Gardenia
Heliotrope
Hoya, wax plant
Jasmine
Michelia, banana shrub
Mitriostigma, African gardenia
Murraya, mock orange
Osmanthus, sweet olive
Passionflower
Piqueria, stevia
Pittosporum, Australian laurel
Stephanotis, Madagascar jasmine
Tabernaemontana, butterfly gardenia
Trachelospermum, Confederate
    jasmine

Not only are the rose-shaped blossoms of Gardenia jasminoides *a pleasure to behold, they're also incredibly fragrant.*

Scented-Leaved Plants

Aloysia, lemon verbena

Centratherum, Martinique bachelor's button

Chamaemulum, chamomile

Lantana

Melissa, lemon balm

Mentha, mint

Murraya, curry-leaf plant

Pogostemon, patchouli

Premna, neem

Rosemary

Scented geranium

Thyme

trumpet, sweet olive, trachelospermum, citrus, gardenia, and hoya, are white or cream-colored; they depend on aroma rather than color to summon their pollinators. But you can find some blaring exceptions. Fragrant orchids, for example, come in all shades from orange to blue. Yesterday-today-and-tomorrow, royal purple in hue, is so fragrant that even the buds are aromatic, and the spent blooms remain scented after they tumble to the ground. Honeybells is vivid buttercup yellow and yet so intensely honey scented that bees seek it out if they can sneak in through an open door or window. A fragrant windowsill will never be gaudy, but a few showy flowers provide welcome relief.

Flowers are not the only sources of aroma — some leaves are also fragrant. Compared to floral perfume, foliar scents are not so blatantly advertised. Most fragrant leaves must be touched or pinched before they release their scent. Fondle the foliage of scented geraniums, and such surprising aromas as coconut, rose, nutmeg, and lemon hit you square in the nose. Basil, rosemary, patchouli, plectranthus, and lavender are other popular scented-leaved plants appropriate for sunny windowsills. Generally native to Mediterranean, alpine, or desert regions, most plants with aromatic leaves prefer bright light.

One word of caution: not everyone loves all flower scents. For example, some people adore the aroma of paper-white narcissus, but others find the scent offensively cloying, especially after dark. Most folks like the scent of night-blooming jasmine initially, but it may become too intense in close quarters. Similarly, prolonged interaction with the fragrance of winter-blooming jasmine can be overwhelming. When in doubt about a scented flower, select a plant that doesn't send its aroma traveling. If you have to touch your nose to a blossom to discover its fragrance, you can rest assured that it will remain unobtrusive.

Working with Texture. Although flowers are the traditional reward for a gardener's efforts, leaf patterns can be just as beautiful as blossoms. And leaf textures can also lend intrigue. Some foliage feels lovely to your touch: many begonias and scented geraniums have soft, velvety leaves, and some philodendrons have satiny foliage.

However, certain plants don't lend themselves to frequent fondling and should be admired only by eye. Venus's flytrap has fangs at the edges of the leaves to trap hapless insects in its jaws. Many cacti and some succulents are barbed with perilously sharp prongs — it's best not to place them in front of a window

that you open and close frequently. If you like the armored look but prefer to avoid being jabbed, choose something harmless like tiger's jaws, which has a shark-wide yawn but no shredding teeth. Or try the old-man cactus, which is covered by a shock of white, Einstein-esque hair.

A Child's Garden. Kids love to grow plants. Of course, you may have to help with the maintenance duties once in a while — few nine-year-olds remember to water regularly. But any child who expresses an interest in plants should be given a few to nurture and a pint-sized watering pot to wield. She or he will develop a lifelong intimacy with green things as well as positive childhood memories.

Children are especially fond of plants with texture and fragrance. They love to pet the long, caterpillar-like catkins of the chenille plant and strawberry firetails. They're fond of the crazy hairdo on an old-man cactus (there's

Where light levels are low, concentrate on interesting foliage textures. The patterns and shapes of maranta, ivy, and Persian shield please all the senses.

The contrast of the ghostly white of caladium against the dark leaves of the rubber tree makes this scene so dramatic you scarcely miss flowers.

no harm in gently combing its white fuzz), and they enjoy fondling lamb's ears. The scents of peppermint and spearmint plants remind them of bubble gum. They love the diverse perfumes in scented geranium leaves and are intrigued by the colors in the velvety leaves of purple passion plant. Willing bloomers such as impatiens give them a sense of accomplishment. All of these plants will remain happy and healthy with minimal care — and low maintenance is the secret to success for a child's garden.

Seasonal Themes. Ever-blooming plants are the mainstays of the windowsill, but a seasonal display offers an element of change; your sill can look entirely different in spring than it did in midwinter. There's a sense of drama in a seasonal indoor garden, for anticipation is heightened as you wait for buds to swell.

Many gardeners are too busy to bother with indoor gardening during the growing season, when the backyard demands full attention. So they cultivate a winter-blossoming garden with begonia, Australian flowering plants (such as chorizema, grevillea, pittosporum, and prostanthera), marmalade plant, winter-blooming jasmine, lotus, winter-blooming buddleia, and amaryllis. The display is fantastic just when they crave the sight of flowers. In spring, when the show is over, they bring their window garden outside under a tree or onto a porch to breathe fresh air and be watered by raindrops. It's the best of both worlds.

You can also display a springtime garden before that time of year actually arrives in your region. Bulbs are perfect for the purpose. Beyond paper-whites, you can force most narcissus to bloom in late winter by prechilling them in the refrigerator for a few weeks prior to planting. In fact, many spring bulbs that aren't usually promoted for forcing will flower if they're prechilled. Hyacinth, grape hyacinth, crocus, snowdrops, chionodoxa, allium, and even dogtooth violet can all be successfully forced. Tulips take longer than other spring bulbs to sprout, and their blossoms last only a brief time before the petals shatter, but you can prolong their performance by keeping them in out of direct sun. In fact, most forced bulbs tarry longer if you keep them cool and protected from bright light. In addition to spring bulbs, primroses and violets enhance the scene. Foxgloves make wonderful potted plants, and their tall spires last much longer indoors, where they are protected from the ravages of spring thunderstorms. Add a few vases of forced forsythia, magnolia, and pussy willow branches to complete your faux-spring scene.

Profiling a Collection. Some people fall in love with a particular variety of plants. They can't get enough begonias, geraniums, passionflowers, or aeschynanthus, and they devote their display solely to members of that clan. Developing such a collection can be educational as well as beautiful. You really notice the subtle nuances among different family members when you see them all side by side. If you choose a fascinating group of plants, you will have plenty of diversity in your display. Furthermore, it's easier to care for plants that share similar needs and wants. Chances are you'll be furnishing drinks in perfect synchronization and fertilizing all your plants simultaneously. The more you study a certain group of plants, the more you learn about their personal eccentricities. Others in your family and guests will also learn from your collection.

Part of the intrigue of a theme garden is the story that it tells. When friends come to visit, you can send them into the front parlor just when all the scented evening bloomers are opening. Or you can explain the subtle variations exhibited in different kinds of begonia leaves. Sharing is half the fun of gardening — and when you grow an indoor garden, the sharing continues throughout the year.

CHAPTER 8:

A GALLERY OF PLANTS

■ *Abutilon* / Flowering maple, parlor maple
Height: 2–3 feet
Exposure: south-facing window
Watering: water when dry
Night temperature: 55–60 degrees

Flowering maple has been a mainstay indoors since the first houseplants were introduced into nineteenth-century parlors. The common name refers to the maple-shaped leaves, which may be green or variegated, but the flowers are the main attraction. If given ample light, abutilons will earn their keep by producing an ever-ready supply of 2-inch, bell-shaped blossoms in shades of white, pink, red, salmon, and yellow. Incredibly easy to please, abutilons can be grown even by a beginner. In fact, flowering maples can be so enthusiastic that they outgrow your windowsill space. Rigorous pruning will remedy that problem. Or grow one of the dwarf varieties such as 'Moonchimes' or 'Clementine'.

If abutilons have a problem, it is that they are prone to whitefly. They may also fall prey to red spider mites and aphids, but both are easily controlled.

The rhizomatous begonia 'Cleopatra' is famed for its maple-shaped leaves.

■ *Acalypha* / Chenille plant
Height: 2–3 feet
Exposure: south-facing window
Watering: wilts easily; keep evenly moist
Night temperature: 60–65 degrees

Definitely a conversation piece, a chenille plant in full blossom is bound to turn heads: its foot-long catkins dangle from the tips of branches clad in majestic, broad, shiny green leaves. The catkins are blush pink on *Acalypha hispida* and creamy white on the 'Alba' form, and they tarry for a considerable time, providing a year-round display. Even if you hate to cut off blossoms, prune the blooming plant anyway; it will branch out and produce more flowers in no time.

Acalypha hispida monopolizes a generous chunk of window space. If you don't have enough room, try *Acalypha repens,* strawberry firetails, instead. It also has shocking pink catkins, but they're only about the size of a caterpillar. Both plants are wonderful for children, who love to pet the fuzzy blossoms.

■ *Begonia* / Rex begonia, angel-wing begonia, wax begonia
Height: varies according to variety, from 6 inches to 4 feet
Exposure: east- or west-facing window; good for artificial lights
Watering: allow to dry out slightly between waterings
Night temperature: 65 degrees

Because of their low light demands, begonias make great houseplants. If you're fond of brightly colored foliage, try the rex and rhizomatous types, which have bands or streaks of silver, blush pink, and green. Although rex begonias have fancy foliage, they don't excel in terms of flowers. Rhizomatous begonias, on the other hand, have both ornamental leaves and astilbe-like spires of pink or white blossoms, primarily in spring. If your home is dry, use a humidifier with rex and rhizomatous begonias.

Angel-wing begonias are easier to please. With their long, wing-shaped leaves and white, red, pink, salmon, or orange blossoms, they'll grow happily in an east- or west-facing window or a south window that doesn't become too bright. Angel-wings range in size from 6 inches to 4 feet. With pruning, most will remain comfortably windowsill-sized.

Abutilon pictum *'Thompsonii', flowering maple, has both ornamental leaves and stunning salmon flowers.*

Acalypha hispida, *chenille plant, spends the entire year clad in dangling, very pettable blossoms.*

The smaller wax begonias (sometimes called rose begonias) don't have the most interesting foliage in the family, but they are smothered in red, white, or pink rose-shaped blossoms throughout the year. They are the easiest begonias to grow indoors.

Few insects pester begonias. All detest wet toes, so let the soil become dry between waterings.

■ **Bougainvillea**
Height: large vine up to 6 feet or more
Exposure: south-facing window
Watering: water when dry; slight wilting may encourage blossoms
Night temperature: 65 degrees

Although bougainvillea is finicky, it is one of the most dramatic vines to grow indoors. Given a bright exposure, sufficient humidity, and warm temperatures, this woody vine will be tipped with quantities of sweet-pealike blossoms in a broad range of colors including magenta, pink, orange, yellow, white, and lavender. Some have variegated leaves ('Raspberry Ice' has cream-edged leaves and magenta blooms), and some, notably 'Thimbra', have bicolored bracts.

Bougainvilleas become big, especially if you allow the branches to go where they want. A better idea is to wrap the branches around a large trellis in a wreath-like fashion. If you're really strapped for space, try growing the relatively dwarf 'Pink Pixie'.

Bougainvilleas will drop their leaves when temperatures dip below 50 degrees. They also object to overwatering, insufficient light, gas from heating or cooking, and low humidity. When a bougainvillea sulks, it usually loses leaves. If the problem is cool temperatures, the plant will often refoliate in spring.

■ **Cacti and Succulents**
Height: 1 inch to several feet, depending upon variety
Exposure: bright south-facing window
Watering: water sparsely
Night temperature: 45–65 degrees

One of the best known of the succulents is flaming Katy (kalanchoe), valued for its midwinter blossoms (left). The most dramatic of the calatheas, Calathea zebrina, *is also the most finicky, demanding high humidity and warm temperatures (right).*

Cacti feature a fascinating array of spines and thorns that seem strangely beautiful. Not all are dangerously barbed; the old-man cactus is soft and fuzzy, and children find its plume of white hair fascinating. Succulents often have smooth flesh, but their leaves are plump water-storage units that are also intriguing. A plus for indoor gardeners is that cacti and succulents prefer a dry atmosphere. And because they retain water, you needn't water them often. In fact, gardeners tend to overwater these plants. Once a week is plenty in the sunniest, driest time of year, and in winter once every two or three weeks is quite ample. These plants are ideal for gardeners who are frequently out of town. Furthermore, they don't take up much space, and most bugs find them abhorrent.

Cacti and succulents all prefer a sandy soil for drainage. Just add one-third part sand to your soil mix when you're repotting — though most cacti and succulents don't require frequent repotting.

■ *Calathea* and *Maranta* / Peacock plant, cathedral-windows, prayer plant
Height: 6 inches – 1½ feet
Exposure: east- or west-facing window; good for artificial lights
Watering: keep slightly moist
Night temperature: 65 degrees

Calatheas and marantas rival begonias in their range of leaf colors and patterns, with all sorts of bizarre combinations of spots and slashes in shimmering colors. And, like begonias, they don't demand a lot of light to thrive. Other than mealybugs, which attack anything, insects are not attracted to them.

All calatheas and marantas hate to have their roots smothered in closely packed soil and would prefer to be potted in sphagnum moss. Although the two plants are discussed together because of their physical similarities (they are in the same family), marantas are much easier to grow. They can tolerate low humidity and will survive with scant light and little care, making them a popular item in the supermarket plant section.

Calatheas aren't quite so forgiving. They demand a moist atmosphere; some gardeners find that they grow best in a terrarium.

■ Camellia
Height: *C. japonica* to 4 feet; *C. sasanqua* under 3 feet
Exposure: east- or west-facing window
Watering: water when dry; provide additional water in late summer when
    they set buds
Night temperature: 40–50 degrees

In the depths of winter, just when you need them the most, camellias open their roselike blossoms. But if you try to grow them in a warm living room, you'll never see flowers. Camellias demand a chilly environment for the buds to set, hold, and open. Even if a plant has promising buds, those buds will drop if the room remains warm at night. Daytime temperatures can rise, but cool nights are crucial. To coax camellias to bud, gardeners set them in barely heated porches, cool spare bedrooms, or breezy entryways. Light is usually not a problem — they tolerate quite low light levels.

Camellias such as 'Anticipation' make impressive midwinter bloomers. They need cool temperatures to set their buds, however.

Because of their immense powder-puff blossoms, made popular by florists, *Camellia japonica* hybrids are more commonly found at nurseries. However, the smaller-flowering *Camellia sasanqua* hybrids actually perform better in the average home, being less stubborn about their temperature demands. Unless the environment is stiflingly hot, buds will stay on and continue to swell when the furnace goes on in late fall. The plants are smaller in stature than *C. japonica* and thus easier to accommodate indoors. And though the flowers are smaller, each branch has many blossoms.

Other than their predilection for cold conditions, camellias are easy to grow. They don't require high humidity, they grow so slowly that pruning is rarely an issue, and they aren't voracious feeders. Mealybugs and scale are the only insects that pester them.

■ *Cissus* / Kangaroo vine, grape vine
Height: climbing or cascading to 3 feet
Exposure: east- or west-facing window
Watering: when dry
Night temperature: 45–65 degrees

Because it covers ground so quickly, Cissus rhombifolia *is known as the kangaroo vine. With its oversized leaves, 'Ellen Danica' is particularly attractive.*

When your children go to college, send them off with a grape vine for their dormitory window. You can rest assured that the plant will thrive despite continual neglect and less than optimal growing conditions. And because it sends leafy arms wandering in all directions, it seems more entertaining than your average foliage plant.

Cissus varieties come in several shapes and sizes; some have leaves no larger than your fingernail, others are clad in foliage reminiscent of oak leaves, but all are vining plants. Grow them as climbers with some sort of support (you don't need a trellis for their featherweight branches; even a string will do — cissus is a tendril climber) or let them cascade downward. Besides keeping abreast of their vigorous growth and making certain that their tendrils don't grasp objects that are off-limits, you can almost ignore them. They seem to be nearly impervious to insects, they forgive forgetful waterers, and they are able to tolerate a very dry atmosphere.

The variegated calamondin orange features both variegated foliage and ornamental fruit. A feast for the eye, the calamondin fruits are not considered to be of table quality.

■ *Citrus* / Orange, lemon, lime, grapefruit, kumquat
Height: 3–4 feet
Exposure: east-, west-, or south-facing window
Watering: when dry
Night temperature: 55–65 degrees

Few indoor plants offer the features that citrus plants provide. From summer through fall, they're adorned by white, intensely fragrant flowers. In the middle of winter, some of those blossoms set fruit that slowly ripens. A citrus on the windowsill entertains over a long period of time.

All citrus varieties have fragrant flowers, and they all remain dwarf if you contain the roots in a pot. Many years will slip by before they become too large to be accommodated in a picture window. Not all citrus varieties will set fruit in the house; the best types for an indoor garden are oranges, lemons, limes, and kumquats. Tangerines and grapefruit rarely set fruit indoors.

Some gardeners try to grow citrus plants from seed. However, most varieties will not set fruit for at least seven years from seed. For quicker results it's better to purchase a rooted cutting from a fruiting bush.

■ *Clerodendrum* / Glory-bower
Height: vine to 3 feet
Exposure: south-facing window
Watering: keep slightly moist; it dries out frequently
Night temperature: 60–65 degrees

Clerodendrums are among the most exciting indoor plants. There are several different sorts, but the best by far for the average windowsill is the glory-bower, which has large, handsome, shiny leaves and is dappled with blossoms. The bright Christmas red flowers peek from balloonlike white pouches like those of bleeding hearts seen in gardens outdoors. They blossom in both summer and winter.

Sometimes called the bleeding-heart vine, Clerodendrum thompsoniae *has balloonlike white flower bracts and bright red blossoms.*

Although glory-bower grows best when temperatures don't fall below 60 degrees at night, it will survive colder conditions. It prefers a bright, south-facing window but will tolerate an east or west exposure. And it takes low humidity in stride. Glory-bowers rarely wilt irrevocably, although they prefer to be watered daily. Because they drink so copiously, they should be grown in deep pots; azalea pots dry out too quickly.

■ *Crossandra* / Firecracker flower
Height: 1 foot
Exposure: bright south-facing window; good for artificial lights
Watering: when dry
Night temperature: 55–65 degrees

Crossandras are the unsung new heroes of the indoor garden. They haven't really been exploited by local garden centers yet, but as soon as the talent scouts find them, they'll definitely become superstars. They bloom reliably throughout the year without fuss, are self-branching without pruning, don't require a lot of water, and rarely need to be repotted. These plants just sit on your sunny windowsill and blossom their little hearts out.

Crossandras come in two colors, both vivid. There's an electric orange version and a finch yellow type, which has silver veins on its small leaves. Crossandras remain tidy for half a year or more with scarcely a yellow leaf, but eventually they begin to look a little unkempt. To get a fresh start, you can take cuttings or grow them from seed. The seeds germinate rapidly, and plants will blossom within a month or two of sowing.

■ *Cyclamen*
Height: under 1 foot
Exposure: east- or west-facing window; good for artificial lights
Night temperature: 50–60 degrees

Perfect for the holidays, cyclamens bloom in the middle of winter and continue flowering for several months in colors ranging from white to all shades of red and

pink. Cyclamens are easy to grow as long as you provide sufficient water to keep abreast of their voracious thirst. If you forget to water your plant more than once, it is likely to slip into a permanent decline. But they also hate to be drenched. It's a delicate balance.

Other than faithful watering, cyclamens require little further care. Just sit back and enjoy the blossoms until the plant is finished flowering. Then the easiest thing to do is toss it out and start over the following winter.

■ *Cyperus* / Umbrella plant
Height: 1–1½ feet
Exposure: east- or west-facing window
Night temperature: 55–65 degrees

Although they don't produce showy blossoms, umbrella plants are far from boring. They send up bladelike stalks topped by tufts of leaves in an umbrella configuration. *Cyperus alternifolius* is a dwarf variety, and there are much taller umbrella plants, such as *Cyperus papyrus*, but their growth habits are similar.

In their native habitats, cyperus is aquatic. There's no need to sink the roots in water at home, but you shouldn't forget to quench their thirst on a regular basis. To keep the soil from drying out, grow them in larger containers than their roots seem to demand. Other than that one caution, they're easy to please. For a dramatic display, line up three or four cyperus in a box on your windowsill.

■ *Exacum* / Tiddly-winks, Persian violets
Height: 1 foot
Exposure: south-facing window; good for artificial lights
Watering: when dry; don't overwater
Temperature: 50–65 degrees

For indoor gardeners who want plenty of flowers with little effort, tiddly-winks is the perfect choice. This cheerful little plant forms a mound of small, shiny green leaves that aren't remarkable, but they usually remain hidden behind a

Its cheerful, year-round blue blossoms have earned Exacum affine *the common name of tiddly-winks.*

crowd of purplish blue violalike blossoms, each accented by a butter yellow beak in the center. Not only are the flowers plentiful and produced throughout the year, they are obtained with little or no effort. Tiddly-winks is one of the easiest houseplants to grow.

The blossoms of an exacum plant will continue for several months of prime impact before going into decline. Then it's time to purchase a new one or start more plants from seed. Tiddly-winks works well in an indoor window box, and the flowers are lightly scented when the sun falls on their petals.

■ Ferns

Height: 6 inches–1½ feet, depending on variety

Exposure: north-, east-, or west-facing window; good for artificial lights

Watering: keep evenly moist

Night temperature: 60 degrees

The Victorians discovered that ferns grow happily in low-light areas indoors, and they've been employed for that purpose ever since. Although Boston and maidenhair ferns are the most commonly grown, they are not the easiest. Boston ferns mope if they're not provided with ample humidity, and maidenhairs go dormant if the temperature dips below 60 degrees just once. Easier for the average house might be bird's nest fern *(Asplenium)*, tree fern *(Blechnum)*, holly fern *(Cyrtomium)*, footed fern *(Davallia)*, and button fern *(Pellaea)*. These all remain conveniently windowsill-sized.

Although ferns don't like dry soil, they don't want to be constantly soggy. Keep them slightly moist but not drenched. Amending the soil with additional peat also helps. Or mix in a few handfuls of leaf mold from the previous autumn's cleanup — it's like chocolate for ferns.

■ *Fuchsia* / Lady's eardrops

Height: 2–3 feet and up, depending upon variety

Exposure: east- or west-facing window

Watering: when dry

Night temperature: 50–55 degrees

Fuchsias are great indoor plants. With little coaxing and not much care besides an occasional pruning to encourage bushiness, they will brighten your east or west windowsill with blossoms. Some plants prefer more light, but not fuchsias; they suffer in a sunny window.

Not all fuchsias bloom throughout the year. The best for nonstop flowering are the burgundy-leaved hybrids — 'Gartenmeister Bonstadt', 'Honeysuckle', and 'Thalia'. The miniature types also tend to produce wintertime blooms in addition to their spring and summer display. Highly recommended are 'Tom Thumb',

Even in low light, fuchsias blossom profusely. 'Madame Cornelissen' is particularly energetic.

'Buttons and Bows', 'Papoose', and 'Bluette'. When the miniatures come into blossom, their branches are dense with little dangling blossoms. It's truly a proud moment. And the display continues for weeks.

Fuchsias don't complain when you let them go thirsty, and they'll recover from a severe wilt without any permanent effects. However, they do grow rapidly, so you'll want to keep the pruning shears handy. All fuchsias lend themselves to training into standards. The dwarf varieties are especially conducive to being trained into a tabletop-sized topiary.

■ Gesneriads / Members of the African violet family
Height: 1–2 feet
Exposure: east- or west-facing window; good for artificial lights
Watering: when dry; try not to get foliage wet
Night temperature: 65 degrees

For gardeners who have only a poorly lit east- or west-facing window, members of the African violet family come to the rescue. If you know this group only by the African violets that your grandmother grew, it's time to explore gesneriads further. Try the cascading columneas that are covered with fiery dragon-shaped blooms in autumn and winter. Or grow Cape primroses *(Streptocarpus)*; their orchidlike blossoms, in every shade including blue, purple, red, nearly black, blush pink, pale pink, and white, pop from a rosette of long, slender, primrose-like leaves. For a tiny space, there are sinningias, which could easily be potted in a thimble. For folks with more room, lipstick plants *(Aeschynanthus)* fill a big chunk of window with waxy red blossoms jutting from equally colorful bracts.

All gesneriads prefer indirect sun. They all need a warm climate and suffer from leaf burn when temperatures dip below 60 degrees; one chilly breeze may be enough to send the foliage into a slump. Gesneriads also complain when cold water sits on their leaves. But if you aim the spout of the watering can carefully at the soil and take pains not to wet the leaves, problems shouldn't occur. Rather than risk ruining the leaves, you can water the plants from below. Fill the saucer with water, let the plant sit for a couple of hours, and then empty it out.

■ *Hedera helix* / Ivy
Height: vining to any length
Watering: when dry; will tolerate some neglect
Exposure: north-, east-, or west-facing window
Night temperature: 40–70 degrees

You won't find an easier plant to host than an ivy. If you have a spot where nothing else will live, put an ivy there and watch it perform. One of its most valuable traits is that it is extremely trainable. Plant an ivy on a wire frame and see

Few plants blossom with the vigor and color range of Streptocarpus, *Cape primrose. 'Sally' has plentiful large, deep blue flowers (left). Hibiscus flowers last only a day, but in a sunny window, there will be plenty of buds to bloom in the future (above).*

how rapidly it covers its support with foliage. In a couple of months, you can have a finished topiary.

There's much more to ivies than the plain green types. Nowadays you can find cultivars with heart-shaped leaves, leaves that look like curly parsley, tiny oak-shaped leaves, or lacy skeleton-fine foliage. Ivies have also expanded their color range to include varieties that have speckled, variegated, silver, golden, chartreuse, and pink-tinged leaves.

Ivies forgive all sorts of neglect, but they will eventually succumb if you continually forget to water them. And when conditions get too dry and they become stressed, ivies often fall prey to red spider mites.

■ *Hibiscus* / Rose of China

Height: 2–3 feet

Exposure: sunny south-facing window

Watering: these are thirsty plants; keep slightly moist

Night temperature: 55–65 degrees

For maximum impact indoors, grow a big, colorful hibiscus. With sufficient sun, the plant will spend months producing buds that swell into gaudy, Frisbee-sized blooms. Hibiscus comes in every shade of the rainbow including orange, yellow, copper, pale blue, pink, red, and white. There are double forms with flowers that look like pompons and single varieties with bands of several hues.

All hibiscus tend to become large. Sometimes plants sold in supermarkets have been treated with growth retardants to keep the height in check. However, that ploy quickly wears off, and within a few months the stems begin to stretch. Pruning, however, is a more successful method of keeping the plant in check. And pruning also encourages side growth, which will lead to more buds.

Hibiscus are heavy drinkers and feeders; they wilt the moment you forget to water. Sometimes they even wilt when the sun shines brightly after a period of rain. However, they will usually recover from a slight fainting spell of short duration. Fertilize them once every three weeks in summer when they're growing vigorously. During the winter, buds occasionally drop when light levels are low. Don't fret; when the day length increases, the buds will open.

■ *Impatiens* / Patient Lucy

Height: 1–2 feet

Exposure: east- or west-facing window; good for artificial lights

Watering: keep evenly moist; they dry rapidly

Night temperature: 55–65 degrees

Some plants are custom made for growing indoors. With its ever-ready year-round supply of flowers, impatiens is a good example. Originally, the only types marketed as houseplants were the New Guinea hybrids. Recognized as winners immediately, within a few years after introduction they were bred to bloom in a broad array of sparkling colors including blue, purple, orange, red, pink, and white. And flowers are not the only attraction. Some hybrid New Guinea impatiens have foliage with blush tinges, gold streaks, and variegation. The first New Guinea hybrids opened only in autumn, but breeders solved that problem by increasing the blossom cycle.

Nowadays the latest novelty is the double impatiens, with flowers that look for all the world like little rosebuds. Or if space is at a premium, you can try the miniature impatiens that never exceed a foot in height. Their quaint spurred blossoms are scaled down, but they open by the hundred, smothering the plant. All the new impatiens have the same cultural requirements as the New Guinea types, except the miniatures, which prefer to be kept 60 degrees or warmer at all times.

■ *Jasminum* / Jasmine
Height: bush types 2-3 feet; vine types trail vigorously
Exposure: east- or west-facing window
Watering: keep slightly moist; jasmines wilt easily
Night temperature: 50-60 degrees, depending upon species

There are no words to describe the pleasures of coming home from a long day's work to the scent of jasmine filling your home. Jasmines are the stuff of which dreams are made. The flowers might not be big or gaudy; in fact, most jasmines aren't much to rave about from a visual point of view. But their fragrance is phenomenal.

Jasmines will tolerate a south-facing window, but they seem to do best with less light, especially during the summer. The everblooming types — *Jasminum nitidum, J. officinale grandiflora,* and *J. sambac* 'Maid of Orleans' — are almost always dappled with small white blossoms emitting a large perfume. Each has a unique scent all its own, but they all have a delightful redolence. All jasmines should be pruned often to stimulate branching — they don't make side shoots without encouragement. They share several traits, but the various jasmines all have individual temperature preferences. *J. nitidum* and *J. sambac* prefer night temperatures that remain above 60 degrees, whereas *J. officinale grandiflora* blooms best when the temperature goes to 55 degrees or lower.

Mandevilla sanderi 'Red Riding Hood' is valued for its reliable crop of lipstick red blossoms throughout the year.

The most famous indoor jasmine is *Jasminum polyanthum,* the winter-blooming jasmine. It blossoms only when days are short, but the display puts other jasmines to shame. If given the proper cooling period, the plant, with its lacy, vining leaves, will be dense with star-shaped white blossoms. To blossom fully, the winter-blooming jasmine needs a month-long period of 45- to 50-degree nights in September or October. The best way to provide this prepping time is to simply leave your jasmine outdoors until just before there's danger of frost. Once the buds are set, they'll continue to develop only if you provide cool nights indoors.

■ *Mandevilla,* dipladenia
Height: 2–2¹/₂ feet
Exposure: south-, east-, or west-facing window; good for artificial lights
Watering: when dry
Night temperature: 55–65 degrees

When a mandevilla is in bloom (which is nearly always), heads cannot help but turn. After all, the shocking lipstick red blossoms accented by a vivid yellow eye are definitely attention-getting. In fact, some indoor gardeners don't want such an uncompromising shade in their homes. So, to fit with more subdued decors, breeders came up with lighter shades such as 'My Fair Lady' in pale pink.

The best varieties for the average windowsill are the *Mandevilla sanderi* hybrids. They all bloom nonstop throughout the year despite low humidity and occasionally neglected waterings. *Mandevilla amabilis* 'Alice du Pont' is often sold in garden centers, but in truth it's not a great houseplant, for it tends to go into a slump in winter unless you grow it in a greenhouse. It makes a stunning garden plant, however.

■ *Passiflora* / Passionflower
Height: vining to great heights
Exposure: sunny south-facing window
Watering: dries out frequently; keep evenly moist
Night temperature: 50–55 degrees

Some people may find passionflowers a handful. These energetic vines do all sorts of acrobatics, climbing up curtain rods before you've noticed that their tendriled branches have clung inopportunely. However, if you provide them with an appropriate trellis and keep up with their roaming ways, you can quickly achieve a dramatic display. The leaves of passionflowers are quite ornamental, but the flowers are truly outlandish. Fortunately, some of the biggest, showiest passionflowers perform quite willingly when potted indoors. If you crave blossoms, try blue-flowered *Passiflora caerulea; P. alato* × *caerulea,* with pink and white blossoms; the red, summer-blooming *P. vitifolia;* or *Passiflora* 'Jeanette', with amethyst blossoms.

'Jeanette' is the only variety that produces blossoms in less than bright light.

Passionflowers are prone to red spider mites, mealybugs, and aphids. And spraying can be difficult when you've got that much foliage to penetrate. Keep a vigilant eye out for trouble, and spray immediately when problems occur. Also, don't hesitate to discipline your passionflower. It's best to wind the branches where you want them to go early in the game. If you rip the tendrils from their support after the vines begin to cling, the buds may drop.

■ *Pelargonium* / Geranium
Height: 1½–2 feet
Exposure: bright south-facing window
Watering: when dry
Night temperature: 50–55 degrees

Geraniums were some of the first flowering plants to be brought indoors because they are so good-natured about performing under less-than-ideal conditions. They'll endure low humidity and occasional wilting as long as they receive bright light. In the depths of winter, zonal geraniums often refuse to blossom, but when light levels increase in early spring, you'll see a superabundance of flowers; colors range from magenta, red, pink, and orange to white. Some zonal geraniums are so double that they seem like a cluster of rosebuds. Other good types to grow include the ivy geraniums, with flower umbels that are just as bright and frequent as zonals but with downward-cascading ivylike leaves. The miniature zonals have all the intrigue of their larger-sized peers but take a fraction of the space. For spring and early summer flowers that look like rhododendron umbels, grow Martha Washington geraniums. Or try pansy geraniums, which look like violas. If flowers aren't your sole goal, go for scented geraniums, whose leaves have all sorts of fruit and spice aromas.

Geraniums forgive many transgressions. But for best results, don't neglect watering for long — their foliage yellows when the soil becomes parched repeatedly. Prune them ruthlessly, especially in winter, and fertilize very sparingly.

■ *Solenostemon* / Coleus
Height: 8 inches–2 feet
Exposure: east- or west-facing window; good for artificial lights
Watering: when dry; do not overwater
Night temperature: 50–65 degrees

Don't be confused by the long-winded new Latin name; these plants are really just the coleus that gardeners have learned to love. You've grown them in the garden, but coleus make great indoor plants as well. And nowadays they come in a number of different colors. There are truly sophisticated versions, with copper leaves edged by a discreet band of chartreuse, as well as the riotous red speckled types. They also come in all sizes. 'Kiwi Fern' and 'Inky Fingers' remain under a foot in height, forming mounds of tiny, brightly colored leaves. 'Atlas' and 'Coppertone' grow to 2 feet or taller. A cascading version called 'Rambling Red' has deep burgundy leaves that spill over the edge of its container. When you need a strong accent to set off the colors of your other plants, coleus are perfect for the job.

The new botanical name for coleus is Solenostemon, *but the 'Picturatum' hybrids remain old reliables for a shady windowsill.*

You should discourage blooming on most coleus, for the straggly blue blossoms don't really add to the show. However, *Solenostemon thyrsoideus* is an exception to the rule; it has boring leaves but wands of sky blue blossoms in midwinter.

Coleus come with one caveat: their attractiveness to aphids and whitefly. Keep an eye peeled for signs of these pests. And keep your pruning shears handy. Coleus need continual pruning to encourage branching.

PHOTO CREDITS

Lynne Brotchie/Garden Picture Library: 55

Linda Burgess/Garden Picture Library: vi–1, 53, 56, 57

Deborah Fillion: 13

Charles Marden Fitch: 9, 14, 19, 90, 95 bottom, 102, back cover

John Glover/Garden Picture Library: 82

Juliet Greene/Garden Picture Library: 2, 58, 68

LaMontagne/Garden Picture Library: 34

Andrew Lawson Photography: 7, 62, 75, 87, 89, 97 left, right, 99, 105, 109 left, right, 115

Tovah Martin: 37, 52, 71 bottom, 72 right, 95 top, 112

Rick Mastelli: 21

Mayer/Le Scanff/Garden Picture Library: 26–27, 42, 85

Marie O'Hara/Garden Picture Library: 64

Photos Horticultural: iii, 11, 40, 41, 45, 47, 50, 59, 66, 71 top, 72 left, 80, 92, 100, 101, 107

Photos Horticultural/Tom Pollard: 61

Friedrich Strauss/Garden Picture Library: 5, 24, 29, 31, 67

Brigitte Thomas/Garden Picture Library: 16

INDEX

Page numbers in italics refer to illustrations.

Titles available in the Taylor's Weekend Gardening Guides series:

Organic Pest and Disease Control	$12.95
Safe and Easy Lawn Care	12.95
Window Boxes	12.95
Attracting Birds and Butterflies	12.95
Water Gardens	12.95
Easy, Practical Pruning	12.95
The Winter Garden	12.95
Backyard Building Projects	12.95
Indoor Gardens	12.95
Plants for Problem Places	12.95

At your bookstore or by calling 1-800-225-3362

Prices subject to change without notice